STUNT PEOPLE

Also by George Sullivan

Anwar el-Sadat: The Man Who Changed Mid-East History
Inside Nuclear Submarines
Quarterback
Great Imposters
The Art of Base Stealing
The Gold Hunter's Handbook
The Supercarriers
Superstars of Women's Track
Discover Archeology
Better Baseball for Boys
Gary Player's Book for Young Golfers
Track and Field; Secrets of the Stars
Run, Run Fast
Modern Olympic Superstars
Amazing Sports Facts
Wind Power for Your Home
This is Pro Basketball
Sports Superstitions
The Picture Story of Reggie Jackson
Better Soccer for Boys & Girls
The Picture Story of Nadia Comaneci
How Do They Package It?
Understanding Hydroponics
This is Pro Hockey
How Do They Find It
Better Roller Skating for Boys & Girls
Home Run!
Pro Football A to Z
How Does It Get There?
Better Gymnastics for Girls
Understanding Photography
Pro Football's Winning Plays
The Beginner's Guide to Platform Tennis
The Gamemakers

STUNT PEOPLE

George Sullivan &
Tim Sullivan

BEAUFORT BOOKS, INC.
New York / Toronto

Copyright © 1983 by George Sullivan and Tim Sullivan
All rights reserved. No part of this publication may be reproduced or transmitted in any form or by any means, electronic or mechanical, including photocopy, recording, or any information storage and retrieval system now known or to be invented, without permission in writing from the publisher, except by a reviewer who wishes to quote brief passages in connection with a review written for inclusion in a magazine, newspaper, or broadcast.

Library of Congress Cataloging in Publication Data

Sullivan, George
  Stunt people.

  Summary: Discusses the work of more than 200 stunt men and women who perform amazing feats themselves in order to keep movie stars unscarred.
  1. Stunt men and women—Juvenile literature.
[1. Stunt men and women. 2. Actors and actresses.]
I. Sullivan, Tim. II. Title.
PN1995.9.S7S84   1983   791.43′028′0922   82-22634
ISBN 0-8253-0129-7

Published in the United States by Beaufort Books, Inc., New York.
Published simultaneously in Canada by General Publishing Co. Limited

Designer: Ellen Lo Giudice

Printed in the U.S.A.   First Edition

10 9 8 7 6 5 4 3 2 1

Acknowledgments

The authors are grateful to the many individuals and institutions that helped in the preparation of this book by providing background information and photographs. Special thanks are due Harry Madsen, Alex Stevens, Victoria Vanderkloot, and Dar Robinson. The authors are also grateful to Kim Kahana, Kahana's Stunt School; John Hagner, Hollywood Stuntman's Hall of Fame; Anthony Slide, Academy of Motion Picture Arts and Sciences; Sam Daniel, Reference Librarian, Library of Congress; Laura Masoner, American Film Institute; and the Billy Rose Theater Collection, Lincoln Center Library of the Performing Arts, New York Public Library.

Contents

Introduction   9
1. Hitting the Ground   18
2. Cliff-hanging   33
3. Western Heroes   46
4. Stunts in the Sky   66
5. More Stunts in the Sky   87
6. Cars as Stars   100
7. "Daredevil Daughters"   118
8. Higher, Faster, Hotter   137
9. So You Want to Be a Stunt Person   157
   Index   174

Introduction

Under blue skies on a bright, sun-filled day, high atop the windswept roof of a tall apartment building, a woman struggles frantically with a man. He is bigger and much stronger than she is. As they scuffle, he forces her closer and closer to the building's edge. She loses her footing and pitches over the side. In horror, she twists her body in the air and reaches for the roof ledge, getting a desperate hold. She hangs by her hands above the busy street.

Then a second man appears on the roof. He quickly subdues the would-be killer and helps the frightened young woman back to safety.

The young woman's name is Kitty O'Neil. She is a professional stuntwoman. In the scene described above, she was merely performing a routine stunt—or "gag"—for an episode of "Baretta," a popular television series of the 1970s.

Kitty O'Neil performs a jump from a 12-story building for the TV show *Wonder Woman*. (*United Press International*)

Introduction

Because her back was to the camera throughout the scene, no one in the television audience would know who she really was, or that she was working as a substitute—a "double"—for actress Lana Wood.

The sequence, although hazardous, wasn't quite as scary as it appeared. Had Kitty missed the grab for the ledge, a thin steel cable secretly harnessed to her body would have saved her life. It might, however, have slammed her against the side of the building as it pulled taut, causing pain and bruises. Even worse, the scene would have been ruined and Kitty would have had to do the stunt again.

Kitty, who is deaf, has performed similar exploits on such shows as "Bionic Woman" and "Wonder Woman." She was featured for several breathtaking moments in the movie *Airport '77*. For a 1980 television show concerned with the *Guinness Book of World Records,* she fell 180 feet from a helicopter into a big air cushion, a woman's world record for a free-fall. She had also held the previous record of 127 feet.

Two stunts that Kitty has performed for television have never been attempted by another woman. One is a frightening car roll-over triggered by a special explosive device. The other, for which she wore a special protective suit, called for her to be smeared with a gluey substance and set afire. The temperature within the suit reached two hundred degrees Fahrenheit before the cameras recorded the scene and the flames were extinguished. Kitty emerged soaked with perspiration but uninjured and smiling.

Kitty O'Neil is one of approximately four hundred

members of the Screen Actors Guild who claim to be stuntmen or women. Of the four hundred, about one hundred do about seventy-five percent of the work, earning from fifty thousand to a hundred thousand dollars a year. A handful earn close to two hundred thousand dollars. Kitty O'Neil is a member of the elite group.

People with skill and daring to perform stunts have been necessary in moviemaking from the very beginning. But up until the mid-1930s or so, most stunt people were untrained daredevils, men and women with more courage than ability. The "do or die" approach has long since given way to a professional attitude, to the careful planning of each stunt down to the tiniest detail, whether it be a high fall, an automobile crash, or a fistfight.

Not that there aren't hazards involved. "Anybody who'd say stunting isn't dangerous, I say they're crazy," states Hal Needham, perhaps the best-known stuntman of the 1970s.

"Buying the farm," is a stuntman's expression. "Taking early retirement" is another. Both mean the same thing—dying. In stunt work, dying is often a possibility.

What personality traits do topflight professionals have in common? They're all brave, of course—but not reckless. Their daring is controlled. They're level-headed. Everything is figured out ahead of time. All the things that possibly could go wrong are considered in advance, and efforts are made to surmount them. "*Doing* the stunt isn't

Kitty O'Neil established a woman's record of 180 feet for a free-fall.
(*United Press International*)

Stunting takes skill and courage. Here Harry Madsen performs a fire stunt. (*United Press International*)

Introduction

what's crucial," says Alex Stevens, a stuntman for twenty-two years. "The preparation is."

They're proud people, even vain. They're honest; you can depend on them. They're independent, yet there are very close friendships among people in the field. "There *is* a closeness among us, and it lasts," says one. "When you do a dangerous stunt, a full fire burn, say, and put it all on the line, you know the back-up men will run in and help if you get in trouble. Nothing could stop them. And you would do the same for them."

In recent years, the status of stunt people has changed drastically. Always before, they had worked almost anonymously. Although the public had some vague idea of their existence, the industry would not permit stunt people to be publicized. There was a widespread belief that it could only be harmful to the industry were the public to learn that screen stars did not perform their own heroics.

When a stunt person was doubling for a star, the set would be closed to the press. More than a few stars objected to giving their "doubles" public credit.

During the 1970s, however, newspapers and magazines began featuring more and more articles about stunt people, disclosing the names of the stars they doubled for and other "secrets" of their work. In *Rollerball, The Cowboys,* and *Mister Gunfighter,* films that date to the early part of the decade, stunt people were given screen credit for the first time.

To some extent, what was happening was simply a reflection of what had been happening to films and filmmaking in general. In the 1960s, movies began to be taken

Introduction

much more seriously than ever before. By the 1970s, the motion picture had come to be regarded as an art form, like painting or music. Colleges and universities offered courses in motion pictures. Movies were used widely in education. The making of home movies became a popular pastime.

As a result, people began to examine films more closely, more critically than before. Stunt people were one aspect of film production that came under more careful scrutiny.

The world of professional stunting received a big boost in 1978 with the release of *Hooper*. Originally titled *Hollywood Stuntman,* the film told the story of the world's

This sensational car stunt was a feature of *Hooper.* (*Movie Star News*)

greatest stuntman, Sonny Hooper (played by Burt Reynolds), and how he meets the challenge of a young newcomer. A tremendous success at the box office, *Hooper* featured a complete catalog of stunts, including a rocket-propelled auto leap across a 456-foot river gorge and a 232-foot fall from a helicopter.

The following year, Kitty O'Neil's life story became the subject of a television special titled *"Silent Victory: The Kitty O'Neil Story."* It was hailed as "impressive drama." Many other network television shows since have been devoted to stuntmen and women and their spectacular feats.

Some people deplore the fact that stunts and stunt people are being given so much attention. Moviegoers, they say, no longer believe in the character they're watching on the screen. Their hearts don't pound. They don't sweat or bite their fingernails. No one says, "Oh, what a horrible thing," any more. What they say now is, "What a terrific stunt!"

1

Hitting the Ground

Early silent films, those that date to the first two decades of the present century, usually concerned either gunplay or horseplay, mostly the latter. When it came to comedy, slapstick comedy, the No. 1 figure was Mack Sennett.

Michael Sinott was his real name. He was born in Canada. His parents moved from Quebec to Connecticut when Michael was seventeen. His ambition at the time was to be an opera singer. He became almost everything else, following a career that took him through the circus, burlesque, and vaudeville, and also included small roles in Broadway plays. On his twenty-eighth birthday, in 1908, Sennett went to work for the Biograph Company in New York City, where the movie business was centered at the time.

Filmmaking was loose and frantic in 1908. Everyone did a little bit of everything. Sennett acted, playing minor roles, such as a butler, a country bumpkin, and a sinister tramp. He wrote some screenplays. He did some directing.

Not only did he gain practical experience, but also he had a chance to learn from D.W. Griffith, another Biograph employee and the first of the great motion picture directors. In his autobiography, *King of Comedy,* Sennett pays tribute to Griffith, saying "He was my day school, my adult education program, my university."

This was a period when movie companies were beginning to shift operations to the West Coast, to a small and quiet Los Angeles suburb named Hollywood. The climate was better there. There was a wide variety of scenic backgrounds nearby—desert and farmland, mountains and seashore. More important, there was sunshine almost every day. Sun-filled days were vital because the film available then was not sensitive enough to permit movies to be made indoors or when the skies were overcast.

Sennett joined in the flight to the West Coast, settling on Edendale, another Los Angeles suburb. In 1911, he was able to convince a pair of businessmen—"bookies," he called them—to underwrite a company that he would head to make comedy films. His new studio, named Keystone, began turning out movies in 1913.

Turn them out it did. Films were short in those days. They were measured in reels. One reel held about eight minutes of film. Many of Sennett's productions lasted only one reel. A two-reel comedy was a major undertaking. But no matter how long they happened to be, one reel or two, films were made at a hectic pace. The story would be written, the film shot and edited, and finished movies

Hitting the Ground

would be ready for distribution, all in a few days. A half-reeler (and there were some) could be made in a single day.

All types of people showed up at Edendale looking for work—wrestlers, vaudeville performers, cops, boxers, grandmothers, acrobats, elephant trainers, pretty women, and handsome men. "If they were funny, I put them on," Sennett said. He also employed dogs, geese, chimpanzees, and lions.

Not only did Sennett direct for Keystone, but he also

Keystone Kops were specialists in races and chases, tumbles and spills.
(*Movie Star News*)

thought up the scripts, helped out as cameraman, and appeared in the films, sometimes as the star. Much of what happened was spontaneous. Sennett would hear that the circus was in town, an automobile race was going on, or a balloon ascent was being planned. Then he, his players, and a camera crew would pile into the studio car and be off, dreaming up the film sequences as they sped toward the event. Once they had done their shooting, they would return to the studio to film other scenes leading up to and explaining the main action.

It was a helter-skelter way of making movies, but Sennett didn't care. "It's got to *move!*" he always said. He believed that for film comedy to be successful a "gag" had to be planted, developed, and set off, all within one hundred feet of film—that is, in less than a minute and a half.

In his younger days, Sennett had always wanted to play the role of a comic policeman. At Keystone this old ambition led to the creation of the Keystone Kops, a madcap bunch of actors in baggy uniforms, who all shared one characteristic: They never did anything right. *The Bangville Police* was the name of the first Keystone Kop film. It was produced in 1913.

Chases, races, collisions, tumbles, and spills—these were the chief ingredients of any Keystone Kop comedy. There were no specifically trained men or women available to do these stunts; that is, nobody was designated as such. Instead, everyone simply did his or her own stunts.

Most of Sennett's stars were well prepared for the feats they had to perform. The chief of the Kops, Ford Sterling, had been a circus clown and a tumbler. Al St. John, one of the original Kops, was a trained acrobat. Many other Kops were former circus performers.

Hank Mann, another of the original Kops, was a sign painter, but eventually gave up sign painting to become a vaudeville acrobat, but work was hard to find. When he heard that Keystone was hiring prospective actors, he took a trolley car out to Edendale. The guard at the studio gate refused to let him enter. That was no problem to Hank. He simply leaped over a side fence.

Sennett hired him to be a Kop at 3 dollars a day, with a guarantee of 12 dollars a week. On days when it rained and they couldn't perform before the camera, Hank and the other Kops painted scenery and did carpentry work on the sets. Hank stayed with Sennett for eight years, eventually earning 125 dollars a week.

Hank would do any stunt that Sennett and his writers thought up and would do it cheerfully. One day he was being filmed in a chase sequence along a ridge in the Glendale Hills above Los Angeles. He was supposed to be pulled from the driver's seat of a fast-moving wagon and land on soft ground.

Al St. John was to trigger the stunt by pulling a pin that would uncouple the horses from the wagon. Once the team was loose and running free, they would yank Hank from

In early one– and two–reelers, the buildings of New York were often the stuntman's playground. Here Carlo Aldini performs.

(*Movie Star News*)

his seat. But the pin got stuck and St. John could not work it loose. Meanwhile, the horses were going faster and faster. When St. John finally got the pin out, the horses were racing at full gallop. They jerked poor Hank thirty feet into the air, "like a kite," Sennett was to say. He descended like a thrown javelin, plowing a trench in the earth with his chin.

"He returned to me in need of a face wash," said Sennett, "but without the trace of a limp."

Hank was loyal. "Boss," he said. "I think we'd better retake that scene."

Another time, Hank and six other Kops were involved in a chase scene along the roof ledge of a three-story building in downtown Los Angeles. A protective railing had been erected, out of camera range, to prevent falls.

One by one the Kops scampered across the ledge, the camera filming them as they dashed by. Hank was the last to go. He leaped onto the ledge and then kept going, bounding up onto the railing. Then he ran across *it*.

Hank was grinning as he trotted back to the director. "You like that?" he said. "Maybe a bonus—huh?"

The director was fuming. "I told you to stay on the ledge," he said. "The camera never caught you for a second."

Somewhat the same approach regarding stunts also prevailed when dramatic films of the day were made. An incident that occurred in the production of D.W. Griffith's *Intolerance* was typical. A monumental film, *Intolerance* consisted of four separate stories, one of which took place in ancient Babylon, one during the time of Christ, one in

Hitting the Ground

France in the seventeenth century, and one in modern times. When combined, the four stories were meant to show man's inhumanity to man.

For the Babylonian sequence, Griffith built a massive set to represent the ancient city. Walls towered ninety feet in height. Huge carved elephants, each in a sitting position, posed atop columns of enormous size. Thousands of extras were hired to populate the city. Even by standards of the present day, the Babylon set was spectacular.

In scenes in which Babylon was under seige, the script called for some of the people defending the city to jump from the high walls. When such scenes were being filmed, the director would gather a group of extras around him and ask if anyone wanted to earn an additional five dollars by making the leap. Those who agreed to do so were provided with a pile of hay in which to land.

Mack Sennett hired the race car-driver Del Lord in 1914. As his first stunt for Keystone, Del drove a car off a cliff, wrecking it in a tangle of flame. He emerged from the wreckage with a grin on his face. Next, he drove a car at forty miles per hour off a pier into the ocean.

For the Keystone Kop series, Del designed a big Kop Wagon that could carry fifteen men. Its heavy body and special brakes enabled the man at the wheel to perform spectacular stunts. The machine would race through the Los Angeles suburbs, weaving in and out of telephone poles, engaging in spine-tingling encounters with locomotives at railroad crossings, and executing stupendous skids. The last often were made to happen by one of Sennett's assistants pouring a barrel of liquid soap onto the roadway.

For later Kop films more sophisticated cars were built. They would fall apart when vital pins were pulled or emerge from crashes twisted into unbelievable shapes.

Not all of Sennett's stunts were as dramatic and electrifying as he wanted the audience to believe. Production trickery was sometimes involved. Take the scene in which a huge locomotive bears down on an automobile that's stuck at a railroad crossing but stops abruptly within an eyelash's distance of the car. Sennett staged the sequence by starting the locomotive at what appeared in the film to be the very last scene, with the front of the engine and the side of the car almost touching. Then he had the locomotive back up while the camera crew filmed it. To get the effect he wanted, all Sennett had to do was run the film backward. In the filming of *The French Connection* in 1971, the director William Friedkin used this technique in depicting the "crash" of two elevated subway trains.

To make an automobile chase scene appear even more exciting, Sennett would have the cameraman crank slowly as the cars went speeding by. Then, when the film was run at normal speed, the cars seemed to be traveling exceptionally fast. This trick is still used in the filming of chases involving cars and other vehicles, and chases on horseback, too.

It was in the Mack Sennett comedies that many of the first professional stuntmen got their early training. Bobby Dunn, one of the Keystone Kops and a specialist in high falls and dives, hired himself out to other film companies as a stuntman after he left Sennett. He did, that is, until one day he slashed his face and blinded himself in one eye doing a high dive into a water-filled metal tank.

Hitting the Ground

Richard Talmadge, who became well known for his all-around athletic ability, did his first stunting in 1919 in a Sennett comedy that starred Slim Summerville. Later films in which Talmadge appeared usually featured rooftop chases and fights atop moving freight trains.

Dick Grace, who was to become one of the best of the Hollywood stunt pilots, began in film work as a property man for Summerville. Bob Rose, a slight, small-boned man, who was still stunting as late as the mid-1960s, got his start by doubling for Mabel Normand, who frequently played the female lead in Sennett comedies.

A great deal of stunt technology came out of Sennett's films. Breakaway furniture and walls made of balsa wood were featured in hundreds of his movies. Sit in a breaka-

Bob Rose, a well-known stuntman of the 1940s and 1950s, received his early training in Mack Sennett comedies. Here Rose is pictured with silent-film star Ruth Roland. *(Hollywood Stuntmen's Hall of Fame)*

Hitting the Ground

way chair and it collapses. Get hit on the head with a breakaway billy club and it snaps in two. Bricks used as weapons were made of felt. Bottles were cast out of plaster of Paris.

Many terms common to the stunting profession today were first used in Sennett comedies. Any stunting feat, from slipping on a banana peel to jumping off a roof into a mud-filled pit, was called a "gag." A fall was a "bump." It could also be called a "Brodie," named for Steve Brodie, who had become renowned for leaping off the Brooklyn Bridge—and living. Roscoe (Fatty) Arbuckle was hailed at the Sennett Studios for "taking Brodies that shook buildings."

A "108" was a Sennett term for a particular type of comic fall, one in which one foot goes forward, the other foot backward, and the comedian does an aerial backward somersault, landing on his back. Ben Turpin, according to Sennett, could perform a "108" on a trolley car, on a concrete sidewalk—anywhere.

Film comedy and stunting stayed wedded for decades. Buster Keaton, the Great Stone Face, as he was called, was a comic genius of the silent films of the early 1920s. *Sherlock Junior,* released in 1924, is one of the best examples of Keaton's enormous talents as a comedian and also as a stuntman.

Toward the end of the movie, a spectacular chase sequence unfolds. The villain locks Buster in the refrigerator car of a speeding freight train. Buster escapes through a trapdoor in the roof of the car and then walks along the top of the moving train, jumping scarily from one car to the next. When he reaches the end, he leaps off, saving himself by grabbing the chain of an overhead water tank, which releases a great torrent of water. He hangs there momentarily while the water douses him, then falls to the track. (In falling, Buster fractured his neck, but the injury was not discovered until many years later when X-rays happened to be taken.)

The chase resumes with Buster running wildly along the road, the villain in pursuit. A motorcycle cop overtakes Buster, stops, and hoists him up on the handlebars. But the cop falls off when the motorcycle hits a bump in the road.

Buster, still on the handlebars, just misses an express train at an intersection. He puts his hand over his eyes and narrowly misses a car without seeing it. He drives straight for a big log that workmen have placed on the road. Dynamite suddenly explodes the log in the middle, and Buster drives right through the gap.

Harold Lloyd, who, like Keaton, worked briefly for Sennett, was another of the great comic personalities of the period. Playing the role of a mild-mannered young man in horn-rim glasses, a straw hat, and bow tie, Lloyd performed so many acrobatic stunts in his early films that he was billed as "The Human Rubber Ball."

"It was all basic," says Dar Robinson, one of the most noted stuntmen of the present day. "You know, we call this business 'hitting the ground.' That's what they did at Keystone. That's what we do today. Sure, we've progressed, but the basics are all the same."

At about the same time moviemakers were packing up and leaving the East Coast for Los Angeles, another change was taking place, one that was to have an important effect on the stunting profession.

Up until 1910, the identity of the individuals who appeared in movies was completely unknown to the audience. They were as anonymous as the figures in a crowd at a baseball game.

Little by little, moviegoers began to recognize certain players and establish them as favorites. Since the names of the players weren't given, the public could only connect them with the studios they represented. Thus, there were "The Biograph Girl" and "The Vitagraph Girl." An early cowboy hero was known as "Broncho Billy."

At first, the studios tried to conceal the names of their players from the public. Producers felt that if an individual became well known, he or she would demand more money.

All this started to change in 1910, the year an independent producer named Carl Laemmle hired "The Biograph Girl," away from the Biograph Company by promising to pay her more money and also to feature her name in connection with any film she made for him. "The Biograph Girl," whose name was Florence Lawrence, became the first movie "star."

When other producers saw fans of Florence Lawrence start crowding into theaters to see her films, they quickly began to establish stars of their own. Indeed, starmaking became as important as film and cameras. By the 1920s, such stars as John Barrymore, Rudolph Valentino, Richard Barthelmess, Gloria Swanson, Clara Bow, and Norma Talmadge, all of whom commanded enormous salaries, were among the best known of all Americans.

The star system helped to make stunt people much more

Hitting the Ground

of a necessity. A studio could not let a star risk injury or worse by performing in a dangerous scene. An accident that injured and hospitalized the star could delay a film or even cause it to be canceled. In some cases, there were millions of dollars at stake.

Whenever a hazardous scene was to be filmed, a stunt person was called on to substitute, or double, for the star.

Some stars shunned the use of "doubles," preferring to do their own stunting. Buster Keaton and Harold Lloyd rarely used "doubles." Douglas Fairbanks, another silent-film star, did his own dueling and sword fighting. In

Douglas Fairbanks was one of the small handful of early film stars who did his own dueling and sword fighting.

(*Hollywood Stuntmen's Hall of Fame*)

later years, however, even Fairbanks used a stuntman for any really dangerous scenes.

Mack Sennett was one of those who resisted the star system, a decision that eventually helped lead to his ruin. Just about every great comedian worked for Sennett at one time or another. Besides Harold Lloyd and Buster Keaton, the list included Ben Turpin, whose specialty was crossing his eyes; Fatty Arbuckle, a big man, 280 pounds, but fast on his feet; Edgar Kennedy, who could boil with rage on cue; pixyish Mabel Normand; lanky Slim Summerville; dapper Charlie Chase; Mack Swain; Charlie Murray; Hank Mann; even Charlie Chaplin and W.C. Fields.

By the late 1920s, most of Sennett's best-known clowns had taken better-paying jobs at other studios. Sennett simply would not pay them the wages they demanded. Sennett believed, not in comics, but in comedy—in the crockery that shattered into a million pieces, in breakaway furniture and walls, in the dive from a rooftop into a rain barrel, and in one car chasing another at dizzying speeds.

Cliff-hanging

For evidence as to how firmly the star system gripped Hollywood, one only has to look at the action serials. *What Happened To Mary?*, starring Kathryn Williams billed as the "girl without fear," was the first. It was produced in 1912.

In action serials, one chapter was presented each week over a series of many weeks. It was shown before the feature film. At first the chapters were complete stories that were linked together by a faint story line. In fact, sometimes they were called "chapter plays." Producers soon developed the idea of ending each chapter with a suspenseful climax, which was meant to lure the audience back to the theater for the next episode.

One frequently used scene was the heroine hanging by her fingertips over the edge of a steep cliff. As she looked down in horror into the deep canyon, the chapter would

Cliff-hanging

end. So often was this scene used, the term "cliff-hanger" eventually came to be used in describing any action serial. Today, of course, it has a much more general meaning, referring to any event or contest in which the outcome is uncertain.

The Perils of Pauline is by far the best known of the early adventure serials. Pearl White starred as Pauline, a trusting young woman who had fallen heir to a sizeable fortune. The plot concerned the efforts of the villainous Paul Panzer to steal Pauline's inheritance, preferably by having her meet her death in one horrendous fashion or another. Throughout the serial, or until the final episode at least, Pauline looked upon Paul as one of her closest friends, despite an enormous amount of evidence to the contrary.

Pearl White performs for a stunt in an early cliff–hanger.
(Movie Star News)

Cliff-hanging

But Pauline, as played by Pearl White, was no wide-eyed innocent. Whether she was wielding a pistol, scaling the side of a tall building, or driving a speeding sports car, Pearl always looked as if she were in control of things. Her offscreen personality matched her onscreen image. Although she was often pictured in women's finery, one got the feeling that she would be much more comfortable in slacks and an open-necked shirt.

Each chapter was built around a different adventure. Pearl was kidnapped by gypsies, blown up at sea by a crazed pirate, attacked by Indians, and tossed off a Rocky Mountain cliff. (The cliff was actually a precipice along the Hudson River near Fort Lee, New Jersey, where much of the filming on the series was done.)

The Perils of Pauline was an overwhelming success, not only in the United States, but in Europe, too. Pearl White became one of the most popular film stars of the day. Between 1914 and 1919, she churned out one action serial after another, nine of them in all.

Pearl did most of her own stunts, rarely relying on a "double." Spencer Bennett, a stuntman of the day, once recalled: "Pearl insisted on taking chances. We used to plead with her that if she got hurt she would cause a shutdown and put everybody out of a job. Usually, though, we gave in to her, rather than lose time arguing."

Indeed, time was a crucial factor. Directors were constantly trying to keep costs down, and doubling delayed production. It took time to dress a "double," instruct him in the mannerisms he was to use, and get him in proper position before the camera.

A Pearl White stunt is aided by a breakaway railing. *(Movie Star News)*

A script once called for Pearl to make a transfer from the running board of one moving automobile to another. Although the cars were not moving fast, Pearl somehow lost her footing and fell in between them. Only quick thinking by the drivers, who pulled their automobiles away from one another, prevented a serious accident.

Another time, Pearl was working along the New Jersey Palisades, filming a chapter that concerned a lighter-than-air balloon from which a big, square basket was suspended. The balloon was permitted to float to seventy-five feet and was then anchored with a stout line. The scene called for Pearl to simply peer over the edge of the basket. In the gondola with her was the balloon's owner, Leo Stevens. He ducked down so as to be out of camera view.

Just as they had completed shooting, the anchoring device gave way, and the balloon soared higher, then began drifting over the Hudson River toward New York City. The director and his crew could do nothing but watch in astonishment.

When the balloon was no longer visible, they packed up their equipment and returned to the studio. Several hours later, someone called the studio to report that Pearl and the balloon owner were safe in Philadelphia. While Pearl later admitted the voyage had some frightening moments, she said she wouldn't have missed it for anything.

When Pearl did use a "double," it was in those scenes that required more physical strength and athletic ability than she possessed. Once the script called for Pauline to cross from the roof of one building to another by means of a wire cable suspended between them. Eddie Kelly, described as "a small man," was called. He donned a wig and a skirt and then worked his way across.

Eddie Kelly happened to be athletic. Sometimes inexperienced amateurs were used to perform difficult stunts —with tragic results. In the last of Pearl's serials, *Plunder,* made in 1922, John Stevenson doubled for Pearl in a sequence in which he was to jump from the top of a bus to the girder of a bridge that crossed New York City's Third Avenue at 72nd Street. Stevenson was a chauffeur. Stunting enabled him to earn some extra money.

Pauline was no wide-eyed innocent. She always seemed to be in control of things. *(Movie Star News)*

Stevenson donned a wig and a skirt and climbed to the roof of the bus, which started making its way through city traffic, gradually picking up speed. When he reached up for the bridge, Stevenson misjudged how fast the bus was going, lost his grip, and fell eighteen feet to the cobblestone pavement. He died of head injuries in the hospital.

After Stevenson's death, the serial was rushed to completion. Pearl returned to Paris, where she had been living, eager to begin her retirement.

The public soon developed an affection for another serial queen, Ruth Roland. Whereas Pearl White seldom used a "double," Ruth Roland was different. She demanded a "double" for any scene that involved even the slightest hardship or risk.

Bob Rose was Ruth's usual "double." He had many different skills. As a teenager, Bob had been a jockey. After an accident put him in the hospital, he gained too much weight to continue race riding, so he took up trick riding, along with motorcycle racing and automobile racing. He also gave wing walking and parachute jumping a try. When he arrived in Hollywood and went looking for work, he was told he was too small to be a leading man. Stunt work seemed like a reasonable alternative.

Rose had a professional attitude about what he did. "I have no fear because I'm not ignorant," he once told an interviewer. "I work out every detail of my stunts, so I know exactly what I'm doing.

"A good stuntman has to be scientific. The men who boast of how many bones they've broken aren't good stuntmen. If they were, they wouldn't get hurt."

When he doubled for Ruth Roland, Rose often wore a riding jacket and breeches, along with a wig, of course. He looked so much like her that he was sometimes used in close-ups. In some of her last serials, Rose appeared onscreen more than Ruth herself did.

In those days, no one ever questioned the idea of having

a stunt*man* double for a female star. It became a Hollywood tradition. In recent years, the growing number of professional stuntwomen have denounced the practice. But it became deeply rooted in the movie industry, and only in recent years has it begun to die out.

In the early days of action serials, there was at least one stuntwoman who came to prominence. She doubled for Helen Holmes, another of the serial queens, and the star of *The Hazards of Helen,* a serial that kept running and running, amassing 119 episodes in all between 1914 and 1916.

Helen's adventures were often concerned with railroads. In *Helen's Sacrifice,* Helen leaped from a galloping horse to a speeding locomotive. In *The Girl at the Throttle,* she prevented a railroad disaster by driving an engine at breakneck speed. In *The Girl Telegrapher's Peril,* she jumped from a railroad bridge into the river below. In *The Stolen Engine,* she leaped from the cab of one engine to the cab of another as the two sped along side by side on parallel tracks.

In the early chapters, stuntmen doubled for Helen Holmes. Eventually, a woman was signed up as Helen's full-time "double." Her name was Rose Gibson.

Rose had been a cowgirl in a traveling rodeo show. She had married Hoot Gibson, the show's top stunt rider, who later became a cowboy film star. Tom Mix, another star of Western films, was one of the show's featured performers. Will Rogers, later to become famous as an actor and a humorist, did rope tricks in the rodeo.

In 1911, the owners took the show to California for the

Cliff-hanging

winter and rented the entire enterprise to the movies. Rose and Hoot began making Western movies for Thomas Ince, a pioneer producer-director who owned his own studio. Before long, Rose was in demand as a stuntwoman.

Rose doubled for Helen Holmes, but when Helen left the studio that produced the series, Rose took over the role. The producers, however, made Rose change her name. She became *Helen* Gibson.

In the years that followed, Rose (or Helen) doubled for such stars as Louise Fazenda, Marie Dressler, Edna May Oliver, and Ethel Barrymore. She died in 1960.

No essay concerning the stunt people of early action serials would be complete without some mention of Charles Hutchison, who was dubbed "The Thrill-A-Minute Stunt King." A daredevil, says the dictionary, is a person who is recklessly bold. Charles Hutchison was a daredevil. He parlayed his courage and daring and what athletic ability he had into a career that quickly achieved serial stardom. Serials in which he was featured were sometimes named after him, such as *Hurricane Hutch* (1921), and *Go Get 'Em Hutch* (1922).

Motorcycle stunts were among Hutch's specialties. He would ride a motorcycle right through a wooden fence. He made motorcycle-to-airplane transfers, standing erect on the seat of his machine as it streaked along the highway at forty miles per hour and reaching up to grasp the rope ladder suspended from the airplane. The first time he tried the stunt it was costly. As soon as he had a firm hold on the rope ladder, he watched helplessly as his five-hundred-dollar motorcycle ran off the road and crashed.

Charles Hutchinson, "The Thrill-a-Minute Stunt King."
(*Hollywood Stuntmen's Hall of Fame*)

One of his favorite stunts was to brace himself between the facing outside walls of two buildings and work his way from ground level to roof level. No net was used. In a film titled *The Great Gamble,* Hutchison leaped across an eighteen-foot chasm between two seven-story apartment buildings.

In the first episode of *The Whirlwind,* Hutchison was to

Cliff-hanging

row a log across the Ausable River in northeastern New York State, with his fiancée, Edith Thornton, riding on his back. When he reached the middle of the river, Charles began to rock back and forth. Edith gasped. "Don't worry, my dear," he said. "I have to make it look difficult. Can't disappoint the fans."

Hutch's recklessness caused him pain and injury with some frequency. He once made a leap from the wing of a low-flying airplane to the sill of an open window of a passenger train that was barreling along at full speed. The villain, following the script, slammed the window shut, forcing Hutch to drop to the ground. When he landed, Hutch dislocated his hip and tore ligaments in his leg.

Hutchinson's recklessness caused him plenty of pain. Here he takes a head-first dive from an open window.
(Hollywood Stuntmen's Hall of Fame)

Cliff-hanging

Hutchison's worst mishap occurred in a scene in which he was to jump from a ballroom balcony, catch a huge crystal chandelier, and swing back and forth on it. The chandelier struck the edge of the balcony, sending a shower of glass into his face. Instinctively, Hutch raised his arm to shield his eyes. When he did so, he lost his grip and fell. He broke his left arm at the elbow and broke his right arm, dislocating that elbow.

Despite such misfortune, Charles remained a fearless individual. "Everything depends on your attitude of mind," he once told an interviewer from *The American Magazine*. "Suppose you knew you could jump up and hang by your hands from the ledge above that door for five minutes. If I offered you a hundred dollars to do it, you wouldn't hesitate. But if I offered you a hundred dollars if you would hang from this window ledge, seven stories above the street, would you do it? Certainly not. You wouldn't try it, because you haven't faith in yourself. I have faith, because I know what I can do."

Lightning Hutch, produced in 1926, was disappointing to Hutch's fans. He was overweight and lacking in agility. The serial lost money. Charles Hutchison was not heard of again.

Action serials lasted through the 1930s and into the 1940s, although their popularity steadily declined. Television finally killed them. Like the early comedies, action serials served as proving ground for stunts and stunt techniques that were to be featured in major films of the future.

The era of the action serial, the cliff-hanging thrills of *The Perils of Pauline,* was gloriously recalled in the film, *Raiders of the Lost Ark.* It was released in 1981.

Cliff-hanging

Raiders of the Lost Ark had poison darts, buried treasures, and an underground chamber with deadly snakes—7,500 of them. It had a car chase and a barroom brawl, a brainy professor, a damsel in distress, and more, much more.

Raiders of the Lost Ark thrilled and dazzled. It was described as providing the kind of fun-for-all-ages entertainment that Hollywood was built on. *Newsweek* praised the film for its "edge-of-seat-style," for its ability to hypnotize kids and reawaken in adults memories of what moviegoing was once all about. Little wonder that *Raiders of the Lost Ark* already ranks as one of the greatest box office successes of all time.

Truck stunt from *Raiders of the Lost Ark* adds to the film's excitement. *(Hollywood Stuntmen's Hall of Fame)*

3

Western Heroes

A chase on horseback. A no-holds-barred fists battle. A spectacular horse fall.

These are some of the basic ingredients of the Western movie. They are also stuntman specialties. You cannot make a Western film without stunt people, and some Westerns require whole armies of them.

Like slapstick comedies, Western films go back to the earliest days of moviemaking. Broncho Billy Anderson was the first well-known Western hero, appearing in hundreds of one and two reelers between 1908 and 1914. Broncho Billy was actually a Chicago businessman named Max Aronson. Big and brawny, he was clumsy on horseback at first but taught himself to become a competent rider. He could twirl a rope skillfully, hold his own in a fight, and even managed to do a stunt or two in some of his later films.

Broncho Billy eventually deserted Westerns to make

Stunts are a feature of every western film. This jump is from *Rocky Mountain*, a 1940's western that starred Errol Flynn.

(Larry Edmunds Book Shop)

feature films. At about the same time he did, another Western star, William S. Hart, was growing in popularity

Hart was the typical "strong, silent" Western hero. Frontier life was always hard and rugged in Hart's films, which were well plotted and interesting from beginning to end. But aside from one or two action scenes, they required almost no stunt work at all. Hart wanted to make what he felt were honest films. Stunting and the use of "doubles" smacked of trickery, he believed. He did all of his own riding, even in his later films, when he was in his mid-50s.

Thanks at least in part to Broncho Billy and William S. Hart, Western films enjoyed a period of mushrooming growth beginning about 1910. Every studio made them. As a result, a steady supply of "real" cowhands was required for movie riding and stunt work.

When, for example, William Selig was preparing to produce a film called *Ranch Life in the Great Southwest* and needed someone to serve as technical adviser, he hired a real expert, a onetime livestock foreman, experienced rodeo rider, and champion steer thrower named Tom Mix. After the film was completed, Mix returned to his ranch.

Born in 1881 in Mix Run, Pennsylvania, Mix had left school in fourth grade, had later joined the army and served in Cuba during the Spanish American War, and had broken horses for the British Army. He had been a federal marshall in Oklahoma and a star performer with the Miller Brothers 1010 Ranch Show. With all of this behind him, Mix was ready to settle down.

But Selig contacted him again, asking Mix if he'd be interested in serving as an adviser on future Western films the company planned and also doubling for the principals in action scenes. Although the job meant leaving his ranch and joining Selig's company in California, Mix accepted the offer. Western films were never to be quite the same.

Mix plunged into the world of moviemaking with great gusto. At first, he was kept busy stunting for the stars at

Selig's studio. He toppled wagons, made transfers from horses to trains, and broke and rode wild horses. For one of Selig's dramas, he wrestled a python. For another, titled *Lost in the Jungle,* he served as the safety man for a scene in which Kathryn Williams, the serial's heroine, was to be menaced by a leopard. The leopard had been trained to devour chickens, and the handler kept one concealed out of camera range. When he wanted the leopard to leap, he would reveal the chicken. But during the scene, a breeze ruffled Kathryn Williams's hair, and the leopard became confused and pounced on *her*. Mix was armed with a rifle, but he couldn't use it for fear of wounding Kathryn. So he leaped into the fray and grabbed the leopard by the tail, pulling him away.

Mix soon began making Westerns for Selig, almost all of them one or two reelers. Between 1911 and 1917, about the same period that William S. Hart was rising in popularity, Mix made more than one hundred films, often serving as director, author, and star. He did all his own stunting.

There was plenty of stunting to do because Mix's films were always action packed, full of fights and wild chases. In 1917, Mix joined Fox, the biggest studio of the day, and began starring in full-length Westerns. There was more riding of wild horses and leaping from high cliffs. Mix also did stunts involving locomotives, race cars, airplanes, and even ocean liners. He paid a heavy penalty for doing his own stunts, for he fractured ribs, both hands, and both ankles, and he broke each leg four times. His shoulders were kept in place with surgical wire, and his entire body was marked with scars.

Western hero Tom Mix performed his own stunts.
(*Hollywood Stuntmen's Hall of Fame*)

Maybe it was worth it. The public loved Mix's films, and not just because they were always loaded with action. They presented Mix as the perfect person. He never smoked, drank, or was disrespectful toward women. He would subdue a "bad guy" with his fists or some eye-catching lasso work but seldom shoot him. The films were authentic in the costumes worn and magnificent in the scenery displayed, for Mix often did his filming in national parks.

There were rarely any conflicts in a Mix film; no serious issues were ever raised. The films had good stories. They had lively action. All said, they entertained.

Mix retired in 1935 at the age of fifty-four. He died in an automobile accident at sixty.

The success of Mix's films spawned a new breed of cowboy star, and the movie screens of America were filled with his likeness for several decades. Buck Jones and George O'Brien, both of whom had worked for Mix, were among the first to follow his format. Hoot Gibson, Ken Maynard, Tim McCoy, Fred Thompson, and Yakima Canutt were other cowboy stars cast in the Mix mold.

The coming of sound in the late 1920s disrupted the production of Westerns for a while, but eventually technicians learned how to conceal microphones in foliage or prairie scrub. Audiences were enthralled to hear the sound of gunshots, hoofbeats, and bacon sizzling over an open fire.

Hoot Gibson, George O'Brien, Ken Maynard, and Buck Jones were successful in making the changeover from silents to talkies. They were soon joined by a great number of new and very durable Western heroes—Gene Autry, William Boyd (Hopalong Cassidy), Guy Madison, and Roy Rogers; John Wayne, superstar, too.

Several basic stunts were common to almost every Western film of the 1920s and 1930s—falling off a galloping horse, riding a bucking horse, and getting "bulldogged." In ranch work or rodeo competition, bulldogging means to leap on the back of a bounding calf or steer from horseback, seize the animal by the head or horns, and wrestle it to the ground. In motion picture stunt work, however, bulldogging means to spring from a fast-moving horse onto another rider, or leap upon a man on the ground.

Film Indians were constantly shooting their arrows into stuntmen dressed as cowboys or soldiers. In early Westerns, this was accomplished by sticking one or more arrows in cork beneath the victim's clothing. Piano wire was attached to each of the arrows. With a quick jerk, the arrows were yanked out of the cork (and out of range of the camera lens). Then the film was reversed. As far as the audience knew, the arrows sailed straight for their target and got their man.

Moviemakers improved upon this technique by having a bow-and-arrow expert actually fire arrows at stuntmen. Of course, those who were on the receiving end were protected with steel back plates or breastplates covered with balsa wood that held the arrows in place. Although champion archers always did the shooting, it took great courage to permit a man equipped with a heavy-duty bow to shoot steel-tipped arrows at one's body.

Fight sequences in early Westerns were almost as common as ten-gallon hats. In a motion picture each fight scene is planned, much in the manner of a dance sequence. All moves are carefully charted beforehand. The action is made to take place within a clearly defined area. Throughout the scene, the stuntmen have to keep in mind the characters each is playing and the meaning of the fight in terms of the story line.

No real punches are ever struck. Everything is faked. "If you watch a motion picture, you will see that much of the action is on a broad scale," Gil Perkins, a well-known stuntman, who doubled for the cowboy star Hopalong Cassidy, once said. "To make a brawl look realistic, you have to use long, looping punches and then follow through. It's the follow through that really gives the desired effect."

Sometimes Perkins would make a mistake and really hit his opponent, or an opponent would hit *him*. "For some strange reason," Perkins said, "when you are actually hit, it doesn't look as good as when you're not."

But even a real punch doesn't hurt, because stuntmen don't tighten up their fists. "I never close my fists and hit hard," explained Perkins. "My fist stays loose so it doesn't hit with any force."

Yak Canutt was a movie stuntman who specialized in Western films and gained widespread recognition and fame for what he did. His marvelous horsemanship and ability to take falls enabled him to perform stunts with relative ease. He improved many of the basic stunts of the 1920s and 1930s and developed others that are now Hollywood standards.

He made the simple art of falling off a horse safer. In performing this trick, a rider's foot would sometimes get tangled in the stirrup as he leaped, and the man would be dragged along and often get injured as a result. Yak developed a special stirrup, called the Open-L Stirrup, that never failed to release the rider's foot as he made his leap.

Yak also improved the method of wrecking horse-drawn wagons. At least one wagon smash-up was featured in almost every early Western. To wreck a heavy wagon, a hole would be dug or rocks piled up in the wagon's path, and when the wheels on one side of the wagon struck, the wagon would topple over. But the system didn't work very well. The wheels frequently missed the obstacle, or when they did happen to strike it, the results wouldn't be so spectacular as the director wished.

Yak worked with the horses' harness and developed a cable rig that automatically permitted the team to break loose and also caused the wagon to turn abruptly and roll over, and it all happened at the spot where the cameras were focused. As designed by Yak, the stunt involved the use of a cable of measured length, one end of which was staked to the ground behind the moving wagon. The other end was attached to a release mechanism that had been fitted to the harness. As the horses and the wagon went thundering along and the cable ran out, the cable automatically triggered the release device and the horses surged forward, ahead of the still rolling wagon.

That was one half of it. Yak rigged a second cable that ran from the horses and over the wagon and was attached to the rear end of the wagon body. Once the first cable had released the horses and they were running free, the second cable pulled the wagon over, actually flipping it in a spectacular fashion.

Yak was kind when it came to working with horses. Few people were in the early days of moviemaking. Indeed, horses were often treated brutally. If the script called for a horse to go over a cliff, the director was likely to force the animal to do just that—go over a cliff—inevitably to its death.

Ill treatment also characterized the method used to get a horse to fall. This stunt involved a device known as a "Running W." It was based on the old cowboy method of getting a horse to obey the command of "Whoa!" The front legs of the horse would be fastened together by a length of rope which was just long enough to enable the horse to run freely. The rope was attached to a second rope that ran through a ring in the saddle. Standing off to the side, the cowboy would let the horse go, yell out, "Whoa!" and then pull the rope, pitching the animal to the ground. After the drill was repeated enough times, the horse would learn to stop instantly upon hearing the command "Whoa!"

For moviemakers, the Running W was heaven sent. Ropes attached to either two or four legs of a horse would be drawn through a saddle ring. When the animal reached a designated spot, the rider would pull the rope taut, and the animal's feet would go out from under him. Whenever a script called for a horse to fall (for instance, as if struck by a bullet in a chase scene), the Running W was used.

Another method was to attach the end of the rope to a stake. When the horse reached the rope's end, his legs were pulled out from under him.

Such tripping devices were very cruel. Countless horses were permanently crippled because of them; or a horse's leg would be broken, and the animal would have to be destroyed. The Running W and the sudden and uncontrollable fall it caused also led to riders being injured. Humane societies of the day cried out against the Running W and campaigned to have its use outlawed.

Almost from the first day he saw it in use, Yak knew he could improve the Running W and put an end to the crippling injuries it had been causing. Yak began by putting a wide band around the horse's belly, and he suspended a metal ring from the bottom of the band. Two ropes ran from the saddle through the ring and to each of the animal's front legs. When the ropes were drawn taut, they tugged the horse's front legs toward the belly. The force of the pull was borne by the saddle, not the horse's legs.

Yak always had the stunt performed on specially prepared ground which provided a soft landing place for the horse and the rider. "I, myself," Yak once said, "rode three hundred Running W's, and never crippled a horse."

Yak was born Enos Edward Canutt in Colfax, Washington in 1896. He gained his nickname in 1914 when a newspaper reporter, referring to the valley in Washington where Yak was raised, called him the cowboy from Yakima.

Unlike many performers who specialized in Western films, Yakima Canutt was a real-life cowboy. He rode his first bucking horse at age eleven. He was a ranch hand at thirteen. He was bronco riding and bulldogging steers with a Wild West show at seventeen. He did some roping, too. He became a champion rodeo rider and broncobuster, winning the title of Champion All-Round Cowboy at the Pendleton Round-up in Oregon in 1917.

Yak's first brush with the motion picture industry was

not entirely pleasant. In 1923, he won the Roosevelt Trophy for his skillfulness as a rodeo rider. At the presentation ceremonies, Yak was introduced to Tom Mix. "I'm making a picture," Mix said. "Why don't you come out and work with me?"

Yak agreed to do so. "Just let your whiskers grow and wear Levi's," Mix added.

But Yak didn't like to go around bearded, so he shaved.

Several days later when Yak went to the set and met Mix, the cowboy star scowled. "My God! You've shaved!" he said. "I told you to let your beard grow."

"Sure, I shaved," said Yak. "Can't I be the outlaw who shaves?"

Mix didn't say anything more. But when the filming began a few days later, the director complained that Yak was too clean-shaven and too nicely dressed. "Mess him up a little," said the director. Mix nodded in agreement. "Why didn't you let those whiskers grow like I told you to?" he said. Yak had no intention of growing a beard, and so he left the movies and went back to rodeo work.

He remained with the rodeo for only a brief period. An independent producer named Ben Wilson saw a newsreel (a short motion picture that presented current events) in which Yak rode a bucking horse and was so impressed with Yak's marvelous talent as a rider that he signed him up. By 1925, Yak had appeared as the leading man in *The Cactus Cure, Wild Horse Canyon,* and *Romance and Rustlers,* all silent films.

For the next fifteen years, Yak continued to be involved with Westerns. Often he was the film "heavy," the villain. But more often he worked as either the stuntman or

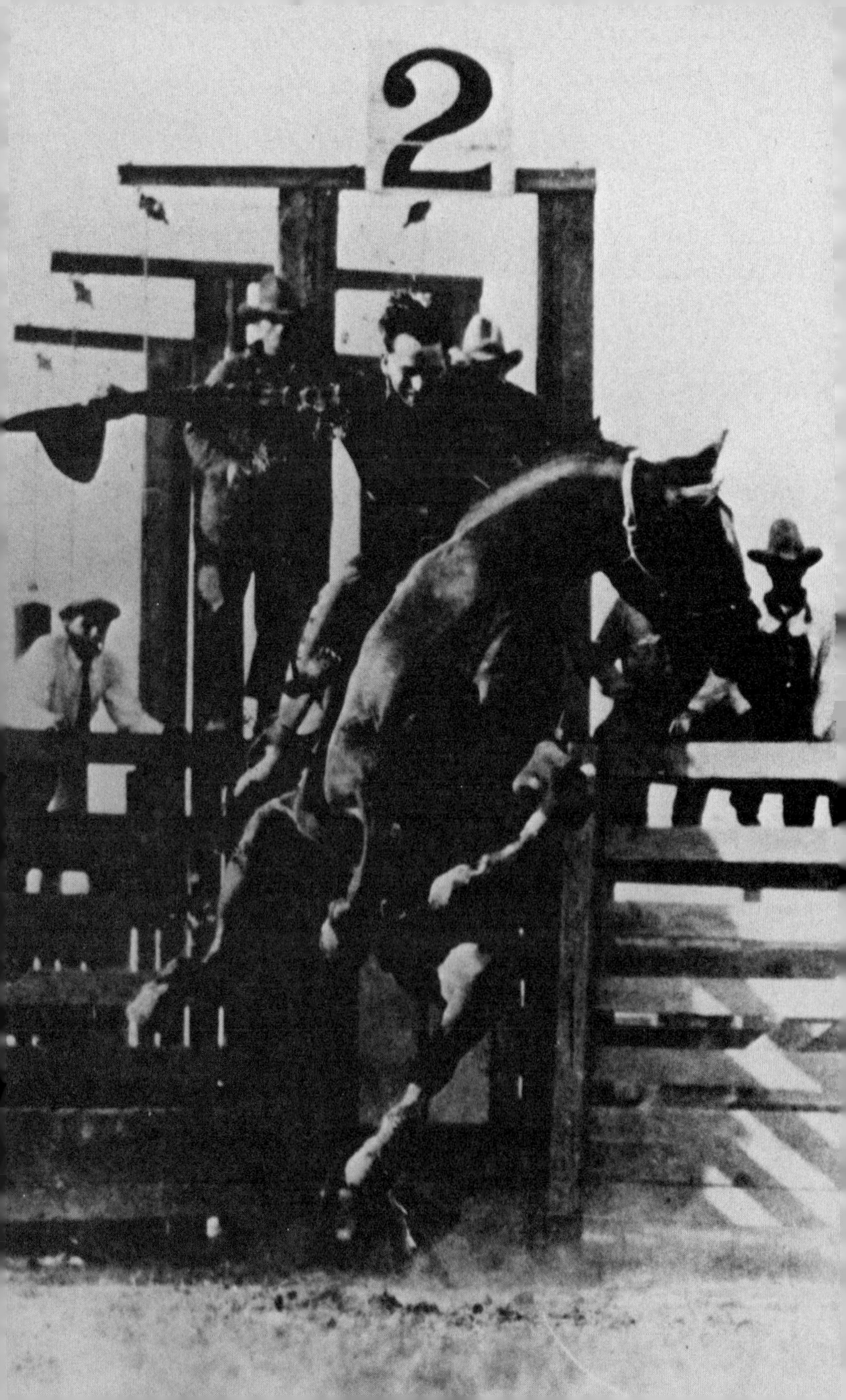
2

stunt "ramrod," the cowboy foreman of the stunt team.

During the 1930s, Yak frequently played the role of the villain in Westerns that featured John Wayne. In some films, he doubled for Wayne.

One extremely dangerous stunt became a specialty of Yak's. It was often used to highlight a film's final minutes. The villain would be attempting to make his getaway by stagecoach. The hero pursued him on horseback. As the hero caught up with the stagecoach, raising one arm to grasp its back, and prepared to leap from the saddle, Yak would be called upon to take over.

Getting a tight hold on the back of the coach, Yak would haul himself out of the saddle, then dangle down in back of the coach with his legs scraping the ground. Slowly, he'd pull himself up, climb to the top, and there have a furious brawn with the villain. Yak also played the villain in these films, which made things a bit confusing. When he doubled for the hero in a fight scene, someone else would have to double for *him*.

After several minutes of fisticuffs on top of the coach, the two men would break apart, and Yak would topple off to fall among the galloping horses. He would slip down between the pounding hooves, hang there for a few seconds, and then let go. As the coach passed over him, he would grab the rear axle and allow himself to be dragged along once more. Then the earlier sequence would be repeated, with Yak slowly climbing to the top of the coach

Unlike many actors who performed in westerns, Yak Canutt was a real–life cowboy. (*Academy of Motion Picture Arts and Sciences*)

and engaging the villain in fisticuffs again. This time, of course, Yak would win. Canutt performed this stunt, with minor variations, for Jack Randall in *Riders of the Dawn,* for Roy Rogers in *Sunset in El Dorado,* and for many other Western stars.

When John Ford made *Stagecoach* in 1939, he signed John Wayne to play Ringo, the starring role. It was this role that helped to make Wayne a star. Wayne asked that Canutt be given the job of supervising the stunts.

The highlight of the film is a wild chase scene in which Indians, riding at full tilt, chase a stagecoach. One of the Indians, played by Yak, jumps from his pony onto the lead horse of the coach team and takes the reins. The driver of the coach shoots the Indian, who drops down between the horses, drags for a moment, then lets go. Then the coach passes over him.

The chase continues. The reins are now dragging along the ground. A passenger, also played by Yak, crawls out between the horses, mounts one of the lead horses, replaces the bit in the animal's mouth, and then draws the team to a stop.

During the chase, the script called for the stagecoach to cross a river. With the help of some propmen from Paramount Pictures, Yak devised several hollowed-out logs, two of which were lashed to each side of the stagecoach to help keep it afloat. Then Yak had an underwater cable fastened to the coach and attached to a truck on the opposite side of the river. The truck towed the stagecoach through the water whenever the horses got tired and stopped swimming.

At Republic Studios, Yak organized groups of stuntmen that he directed in mass-action scenes. He staged the escape from the prairie fire in *Dakota,* the dash of oil-laden wagons through a blazing canyon in *Old Oklahoma,* and the Battle of San Jacinto in *Man of Conquest.* In the last film, Yak helped out by taking three falls from horses.

Yak also kept busy at other studios, doubling for stars such as Errol Flynn in *They Died With Their Boots On,* Tyrone Power in *Jesse James,* Henry Fonda in *The Trail of the Lonesome Pine,* and Clark Gable in *San Francisco* and *Gone With the Wind.*

Just as John Wayne had Yak doubling regularly for him, other cowboy film heroes of the 1930s and 1940s had their own "doubles," men who worked with them on a routine basis as they turned out film after film. Stuntmen and the stars they doubled for included: Gil Perkins—William Boyd; David Sharpe—Guy Madison; Cliff Lyons—Buck Jones; Fred Graham—Roy Rogers; Ken Cooper—Gene Autry.

David Sharpe was a stuntman who specialized in acrobatics, in falling from horses or any other kind of leap, and in high dives. In *The Perils of Nyoka,* one of the most frantic serials ever made, Sharpe doubled for almost everyone in the cast, including the women. He looked so much like Guy Madison, whom he doubled for in a series of Wild Bill Hickok Westerns, that he could be photographed almost in close-up for the star.

Cliff Lyons regularly doubled for Buck Jones, and he also doubled and stunted for other Western heroes such as Ken Maynard, William Boyd, and Johnny Mack Brown.

Yak doubled regularly for film star John Wayne.
(*Academy of Motion Picture Arts and Sciences*)

Exceptionally skilled as a trick rider, Lyons could sometimes be recognized in films because of his distinctive riding style in which he hunched forward slightly and tilted his face skyward.

Ken Cooper and Gene Autry had one of the most enduring working relationships in screen history. During the 1930s and 1940s, Autry films were produced routinely, one after another. As Autry got older Cooper aged right along with him.

Unlike many of his colleagues, Yak Canutt had no wish to make a lifelong career of stunting. He quit stunt work in 1945 to become a second-unit director, staging and directing action sequences that were inserted in the final picture. Like any second-unit director, Yak had his own camera crews and staff of assistants.

Yak directed the battle scenes in *Ivanhoe, Knights of the Round Table,* and *King Richard and the Crusaders.* He also directed the Trojan War sequences in *Helen of Troy.*

One of Yak's most notable productions was staging the violent chariot race in *Ben Hur,* which was released in 1959. The picture was filmed mainly in Rome. The script called for nine chariots to race. Each chariot was pulled by a matched four-horse team. One problem that Yak faced was a horse shortage. There simply weren't enough horses available in Italy. He ended up buying seventy horses in Yugoslavia, and another eight in Sicily.

Ben Hur himself, as played by Charlton Heston, was to drive a team of white horses in the race. The villainous Mesala, played by Stephen Boyd, drove black horses. Ben Hur was to win the race. But when the teams were harnessed up and put through their paces, the black horses always outran the white ones. Since Yak couldn't rewrite the script and have Mesala beat Ben Hur, he installed lead weights in the black horses' chariot to slow them down.

The race, which lasted twelve minutes on film, took twelve days to shoot. It required thirty-eight pages of script to describe the race and all that was to happen.

Canutt trained Charlton Heston and Stephen Boyd in how to handle their four-horse teams. He brought in several topflight stuntmen to double in the most dangerous sequences. These included Joe Canutt, Yak's son, who doubled for Charlton Heston, and Joe Yrigoyen, Stephen Boyd's "double."

For the pile ups that occurred during the race, Yak adapted the harness and cable rig that he used in staging wagon wrecks in Western films many years before. Crashes could thus be staged on cue.

In one of the major scenes of the film, Ben Hur, his path blocked by two crashed chariots, sends his team and chariot leaping over the wreck. It was not to be a real leap, however: The horses were to race up and over a ramp, giving the appearance that they had bounded into the air. The movie audiences would never see the ramp because it was blocked from the camera's view by the chariot wreckage. Joe Canutt was to drive the chariot.

When all was ready, Yak signaled Joe to start his team moving. Joe circled the track to build up speed. As the chariot careened into the final turn and the horses pounded for the ramp, Yak could see that Joe was in trouble. "You're going too fast!" Yak shouted. The chariot hit the ramp and snapped into the air. Joe tried to cling to the chariot's handrail, but he was thrown to the ground and badly shaken. Several stitches were required to close a gash in his chin.

Later, when the footage of the sequence was screened, everyone agreed it was breathtaking. So subsequent scenes were rewritten to match it. After the scene in which he is thrown from the chariot, a bruised and bleeding Ben Hur is shown jumping into another chariot, which he then rides to victory.

Yak Canutt's accomplishments in motion pictures did not go unnoticed. In 1967, at the Thirty-Ninth Academy Awards presentation, Yak received an Honorary Academy Award which saluted him not only for his exploits as a stuntman, but also for ingenuity in developing safety devices to protect stunt people. No other stunt person had ever been so honored.

At a dinner in his honor in 1978, Yak was hailed as "the greatest stuntman alive" by Charlton Heston. "Yak taught us the nuts and bolts of our business," said another veteran stuntman, Jack Williams. "He developed methods to do stunts safely. There's probably not a bone in his body that hasn't been broken. But once he learned how to do a stunt, he did it right. You were assured that nothing was done to a horse or man that would hurt that horse or man."

Yak Canutt was part of an era that has passed. There are no movie cowboys today. John Wayne, who died in 1979, was the last of them. Instead, today there are actors who occasionally appear in Westerns—Burt Reynolds, Marlon Brando, and Lee Marvin, to name a few. Stuntmen don't mind the change. Reynolds, Brando, and Marvin need doubling just as much as the "real" cowboys ever did, perhaps even more so.

4

Stunts in the Sky

The movies and the airplane grew up together.

In 1903, the year that the Wright brothers first achieved powered flight, a significant event occurred in the motion picture industry when a film called *The Great Train Robbery* appeared. Cameras and film projection equipment had been introduced not many years before, in 1895. The novelty of seeing real things in motion—acrobats, parades, and speeding locomotives—left people breathless.

It was not until *The Great Train Robbery,* however, that the motion picture's power in telling a story was first realized. *The Great Train Robbery* concerned a mail train hold up, the formation of a posse to pursue the gunmen, and the robbers' eventual destruction. The film covered all of this despite being only eight minutes in length.

In most previous attempts to tell a story, cameras merely photographed stage action. The result was a play on film.

Early airplane stunts were often filmed by "Jersey" Ringel.
(*Library of Congress*)

But *The Great Train Robbery,* the work of the director-photographer Edwin S. Porter, introduced new techniques in the placement of cameras and the arrangement of scenes. It was the first "real" movie.

People everywhere were thrilled by *The Great Train Robbery* and flocked to see it. "Overnight," says Arthur Knight in *The Liveliest Art,* "the movies became the poor man's theater."

In the years that followed *The Great Train Robbery,* drastic changes took place in the film industry. D. W. Griffith, who has been called "The Father of Film Technique," introduced effects that helped to lift moviemaking to an art form. His film, *The Birth of a Nation,* took audiences by storm.

These were the years in which the comedies of Buster Keaton and Charlie Chaplin poured from the studios and Western films became popular throughout the world. By the end of World War I, the American film business, firmly planted in Hollywood, was on its way to becoming a multimillion-dollar industry.

Aviation did much growing up in those years, too. But whereas movies became big business after World War I, interest in aviation declined. The Army Air Force, suddenly left with hundreds of surplus airplanes, most spindly Jennies and Standards, began selling them on the open market, some for as little as six hundred dollars brand new.

At the same time that airplanes were available, so were pilots. Men in their twenties who had been trained to fly resigned in great numbers from the Army Air Corps. Some of these young men became airmail pilots. Many others took up stunt flying, giving exhibitions in country towns and rural areas. They were known as barnstormers.

This was a time before airplanes were equipped with radios or other navigation aids. Barnstormers often got to where they wanted to go by following railroad tracks. At sundown or when bad weather threatened, they would land in a convenient field. The plane would be sheltered by parking behind a farmer's barn. Out of this practice, the term "barnstormer" came.

The barnstormer's basic stunt repertoire included loops and dives, two-turn spins, slow rolls and snap rolls, and a maneuver called the chandelle, a sudden, steep, climbing turn. There was also the flying leaf, in which one's plane was made to drop earthward in a gentle leaflike descent.

Everyone knew the Immelmann turn, a method of gaining altitude while turning to fly in the opposite direction. Named after Max Immelmann, a German World War I aviator, the maneuver began with the pilot executing a half-loop at the end of which came a half-roll (necessary to put the plane on a normal right-side-up course).

Barnstormers would offer rides to townfolk for one dollar or five dollars or a penny a pound. Sometimes they derived most of their income from getting people to go for rides.

They would also travel in groups, staging air circuses. Parachute jumping would be demonstrated, and wing walkers would entertain.

Quick, light, "with steel traps for hands," as *Flying* once observed, wing walkers were incredible performers. Each had his or her own specialty. A headstand on the upper wing, sometimes only inches away from the spinning propeller, was one standby. Hanging from a rope by the teeth was another, a stunt aided by a concealed harness worn under one's shirt. Earl Burgess would stage a wrestling match with a dummy. Gladys Ingle gave an archery demonstration, standing at the tip of one wing and shooting arrows toward a target set up at the other tip.

It was inevitable that the barnstormers would discover Hollywood. When they did, the result was some of the most spectacular films ever produced.

Many barnstormers earned their first movie paychecks for stunts done for newsreels. When the events happened to be dull, some excitement would be added to the reel by filming a pilot performing dangerous stunts. He might circle down and fly into a hangar and then zoom out the other side, or he might fly under a bridge and then execute assorted aerial acrobatics.

"Fearless Freddie," a Hollywood stuntman of the 1920s, clings to a rope ladder slung from a plane before dropping to the roof of an automobile. *(Library of Congress)*

An extremely popular stunt in silent films involved picking off a stuntman from a speeding motorcycle by means of a rope ladder suspended from a low-flying plane. "The only way to do it," the stuntman Joe Bonomo once said, "was to have perfect timing and an expert pilot who could maneuver his plane so he would be moving at approximately the same speed as you and the motorcycle. Then you took hold of the ladder and simply allowed the plane to lift you up."

The *Skywayman,* the story of an aerial bandit, produced in 1920, was one of the first full-length films to feature airplane stunts. The pilot who did the stunts, Omar Locklear, was well known at the time. As Lt. Locklear, an instructor in the Army Air Corps, he had earned a reputation for rash behavior in the air. When, during a training flight, the radiator cap of his Jenny blew off, Locklear climbed out onto the upper wing and stuffed a rag into the hole to stop the boiling water from blowing back into the cockpit. Another time, he demonstrated his plane's ability to bear the weight of extra machine guns by leaving the cockpit in midair and walking to the end of each wing. He became so confident that he used to crawl down to the spreader bar in between his plane's wheels and hang there by his knees, enjoying the view.

In May 1919, not long after he had resumed civilian life, Locklear formed a barnstorming team with two friends, Lt. Shirley Short and Milton "Sheets" Elliot. The trio arrived in Los Angeles late in 1919, hoping to find work as movie stunt fliers.

That year Locklear and Elliot worked on *The Great Air*

Stunts in the Sky

Robbery, in which Locklear changed from one plane to another at an altitude of twenty-five hundred feet. In another scene, he dropped from an airplane to the roof of a speeding train.

The script for *The Skywayman* called for Locklear to perform every aerial stunt he knew. These included a scary plane-to-plane transfer and a nighttime wing-walking sequence aided by the use of searchlights.

The most hazardous stunt of all, also to be shot at night, was a scene in which the aerial bandit's plane was to spiral to the ground around a slowly descending flare that was meant to represent a robbery victim who was parachuting to safety. Heavy lights were mounted on the wing tips of Locklear's plane to add drama to the scene. Sheets Elliot was to go along as copilot.

Not long after sunset on the evening of August 2, 1920, the group of pilots and technicians assembled at an airfield that the producer Cecil B. De Mille had opened at the corner of Melrose and Fairfax Avenues in Los Angeles. It was ten o'clock when Locklear headed his plane down the runway and into the air. He climbed to about three thousand feet and then glided down to two thousand feet, which brought him within camera range. From below a pair of blinding searchlights picked up the plane, which shone silvery against the black sky. Locklear signaled that he was ready and switched on the wing-tip lights.

Then Locklear dropped the flare that was to represent the victim parachutist and dipped the plane into a tight spin. One observer recalled the gleaming beauty of the spinning wings as the plane twirled about the falling flare.

About two hundred feet from the ground, something

went wrong. One theory has it that Locklear mistook lights on the top of a nearby oil derrick for ground lights, or it may have been that he was blinded by the big searchlights and believed himself to be closer to the ground than he actually was. Whatever the reason, Locklear suddenly jerked the plane out of its spin, whereupon it nosed over, plunged to the ground, and burst into flames. Elliot managed to escape with minor burns, but Locklear's body was burned beyond recognition. His identity was established by a bracelet he always wore.

There was no period of mourning—quite the opposite. The producers of *The Skywayman* hurried to complete the film, eager to cash in on the publicity caused by the crash. There was no shortage of stuntmen willing to take over for Locklear, and Ted McLaughlin was signed as his replacement.

McLaughlin completed *The Skywayman* without any mishaps. But a few weeks later he was performing a plane-to-plane transfer for another film when the ladder on which he was descending swung into the propeller. He had forgotten one of Locklear's safety measures, that of using a rope to tie the ladder to the tail skid to keep it vertical. The oversight proved fatal.

During the 1920s and most of the 1930s, short and stocky Dick Grace reigned as the "King of the Stunters," a term he liked to use in describing himself. From North Dakota, Grace enlisted in the Army Air Corps at eighteen and had flown in France during World War I. After he was discharged, and a barnstorming team he had formed proved unsuccessful, he drifted to Hollywood.

Though Grace would later brag that he never landed a

plane in one piece, his early stunt work involved every type of "gag" except flying. He worked hard at his craft. He sought out acrobats who would teach him the basics of tumbling and falling. He studied the technical aspects of how to skid an automobile by racing his own car along empty streets of Los Angeles and slamming on his brakes at every intersection.

But Grace found stunt work too painful, and the pay was poor. One stunt called for him to jump from the eighth floor of a burning building into a safety net. The men with the net, however, were unable to get close to the building because of the flames. Grace first had to drop to some telephone wires and then swing from the wires to the net. For this he received the standard stuntman's fee of the day—twenty-five dollars.

In another film, Grace had to make a bone-jarring leap from a taxicab onto a concrete sidewalk. After he did it the first time, the director made him repeat the stunt. Then he had to do it again and again—four times in all. After that experience, Grace made up his mind he would start concentrating on the more spectacular stunts, such as leaps of fifty feet or more, automobile and airplane crashes, and plane-to-plane transfers. He felt that these stunts, when planned properly, were no more hazardous than the stunts he had been doing, and they paid much better.

After the death of Omar Locklear, Hollywood studios were hesitant about filming aerial stunts. But Grace managed to convince one producer after another that such stunts could be performed safely.

His first airplane stunt was a simple crash, one in which

he tipped a taxiing plane up onto its nose, then flipped it over on its back. He was much more spectacular in doubling for the cowboy star Tom Mix in a thriller called *Eyes of the Forest,* produced in 1923. At full throttle, Grace flew a Jenny into the side of a barn and walked away unharmed. Before long, almost every studio in Hollywood was clamoring for his services.

Locklear had a reckless streak, but Grace was much more the craftsman, the professional. Each stunt he performed was carefully planned and every safety precaution observed.

He would never wear boots when performing a stunt, preferring sneakers or street shoes. Boots were too hard to get off if you broke a foot or a leg. When Grace crash-landed a plane, special belts held him securely to his seat. Instruments that might cut or injure him were padded. The cockpit was reinforced with steel bars.

Grace totally rebuilt any plane he planned to crash. The main structural parts were sawed half-through so they would break in two easily on impact. The gasoline tanks were moved away from the cockpit. Just before takeoff, the tanks were drained of all gasoline except the amount necessary for the flight.

Grace always had a highly trained rescue unit standing by when he was going to perform a hazardous stunt. Besides a doctor and a nurse, the team included fire fighters and workmen with heavy-duty cutting tools.

This is not to say that Grace wouldn't take chances. Indeed he would, if the price were right. For instance, the standard method of performing a plane-to-plane transfer was to use a rope ladder. But Grace, in a film titled *Wide Open*, did it as a free-fall.

The stunt required the utmost precision. Art Goebel, a highly skilled flier of the day, piloted the plane from which Grace was to make the fall. Frank Tomick, also an excellent pilot, was to be at the controls of the lower plane. A third plane, the camera plane, was to be piloted by Frank Clarke.

When the three planes were airborne and in formation, Grace climbed out onto the lower wing of his plane and made his way to the wing tip. He checked to see that the camera plane was in position. The angle was perfect. He could see the cameraman standing up in the rear cockpit, one eye at the viewfinder, his hand on the crank, ready to start grinding.

Grace then signaled Tomick to ease the lower plane forward. As soon as it was in position, Grace swung underneath the wing of his plane and locked his lower legs around the bamboo skid attached to the wing tip. He then let his hands go and just hung there, his head and arms pointing toward the ground. The wind whipped at his clothing. The engine's clatter assaulted his ears. He twisted his head from side to side, watching the pilots of the other planes as they made their last-second adjustments.

When the nose and leading edge of Tomick's plane was almost directly below him, Grace unlocked his legs and let his body slide toward the ground. If he had miscalculated, he would have dropped almost half a mile before stopping. For a split second as he fell, Grace thought he had misjudged and dropped too soon, and that he was going to fall in front of Tomick's plane by more than a foot instead of a few inches. But as he passed the front edge of Tomick's upper wing, he swung his right hand back and managed to get his forefinger and middle finger around one of the strut wires that connected the two wings. His body flipped over, but the two fingers held. Then, with a sudden jolt, his feet hit a second strut wire.

The rest was easy. He took a firm grip with both hands on the strut wires and got his feet solidly planted. Minutes later, he was back on the ground and joking with his friends.

In 1922, the most active stunt pilots of the day founded an organization called the Thirteen Flying Black Cats. For publicity purposes, they sometimes referred to the group as the Suicide Club.

The Black Cats established a pay scale for various stunts. These were among the typical charges:

Airplane-to-airplane transfer	$100
Airplane-to-car transfer	$150
Upside-down flying	$100
Upside-down flying with a fight on upper wings one man knocked off	$225
Airplane crash	$1,200
Spin to earth with smoke pots	$1,200
Blow up plane in air with bail out	$1,500

One member of the group, Oliver Bontellier, liked to jokingly refer to himself as the highest paid of all Hollywood writers. He received one thousand dollars for every five minutes he worked at his craft. Bontellier was a

Airplanes were the real stars of *Wings*. (*Movie Star News*)

skywriter, tracing words against the sky with chemically produced smoke.

Many of the Black Cats found employment in the production of *Wings,* a 1927 Paramount film, and up to that time the biggest flying film every made.

Wings told the story of two young men, played by Buddy Rogers and Richard Arlen, who joined the Air Corps at about the time the United States entered World War I. The two men become close friends while learning how to fly. The dramatic high point of the story occurs when Rogers mistakenly shoots down his friend, who is attempting to return to his base in a stolen German airplane after having crashed in enemy territory.

Stunts in the Sky

The real stars of *Wings* were the airplanes. Never before, and seldom since, has the military cooperated so wholeheartedly in the making of a film. The Army contributed two air bases near San Antonio, Texas for the use of the film and let the director William Wellman borrow planes and men to fly them.

Wellman, the only director in Hollywood who had flying experience from World War I, devised a system of taking close-ups of fliers in the air by installing cameras in airplane cockpits. These captured the sense of the airplane's speed and motion.

Wellman also figured out how to establish the speed of an airplane traveling fast in the sky. Motion on the screen is a relative thing. When a horse runs, for instance, we know it is going fast because of its relationship to the ground.

Wellman depicted planes as being fast-moving by depicting them in relation to clouds. However, clouds wouldn't always appear when needed. Waiting for them could add many thousands of dollars to a film's cost.

For the two most important stunts in *Wings*, Wellman hired Dick Grace. One of the stunts involved crash-landing a Spad, which was a French plane. The other was more difficult. Grace had to pile up a heavy German Fokker bomber just as it was leaving the ground.

The Spad crash went off without any problems. Grace then began preparing the Fokker, half-sawing through vital frame parts, including the main wing spar, several wing struts, and the landing gear, so that they would collapse on impact.

Grace raced the big plane down the runway, got it into the air, and, as he had planned, swerved and dug the left wing tip into the ground. The wing started buckling instantly, but the landing gear somehow remained intact. The ship bounced back up into the air, and then came down heavily on its nose. The straps holding Grace snapped and his head went through the instrument panel. When he was pulled out of the wreckage, he seemed uninjured except for cuts. He was photographed smiling in front of the wreckage.

Later, however, Grace collapsed and was rushed to the hospital. X-rays revealed he had broken his neck, that actually four vertabrae had been crushed and a fifth dislocated. Doctors told him that he would be bedridden for months and his neck would be in a cast for a year. But six weeks later, wearing only a brace to support his neck, Grace was back flying.

Wings was acclaimed far and wide. "*Wings* is a technical triumph," wrote one reviewer. "It piles punch upon punch until the spectator is almost nervously exhausted." Audiences loved the realism of *Wings*. The film ran for a year and a half in New York and six months in Los Angeles.

On May 16, 1929 when the Academy Awards were presented for the first time, *Wings* was named Best Picture. It has since been hailed for offering "the kind of red-blooded entertainment with which the motion picture industry first found its mass audience and support."

At about the same time that *Wings* was being released to theaters, an even more lavish flying film was being planned—*Hell's Angels*. Howard Hughes, twenty-three, already a millionaire many times over, was its producer.

Hughes spent hundreds of thousands of dollars assembling a huge fleet of aircraft. Besides American planes of the day, surplus Spads, and Fokker bombers, Hughes agreed to lease a big twin-motor Sikorsky transport. He had the ship painted to resemble a German Gotha bomber. Hughes turned an alfalfa farm in the San Fernando Valley into a complete airport, naming it Caddo Field after his production company. He also built or leased seven other airfields in the Los Angeles area.

As production got underway, one accident followed another. The veteran stunt pilot Al Johnson was burned to death when his plane slammed into telephone wires. Phil Phillips had to make a forced landing in a ditch during a takeoff when his engine failed. He suffered a broken neck. Al Wilson was flying a Fokker over Los Angeles when its propeller flipped off. Wilson bailed out, landing safely on a housetop.

In the film's last big scene, the Gotha bomber was to spin straight into the ground after a collision with German fighters. The pilot was to put the plane into its dive and then, seconds before the crash, bail out. Finding a pilot to do the stunt was a problem for Hughes. The owner of the plane, Roscoe Turner, the most successful barnstormer of the day, refused to do the stunt, saying the plane couldn't take the strain. He felt sure the wings would come off.

Dick Grace was approached. Grace said he would do the stunt, but only if Hughes agreed to pay him ten thousand dollars if he survived. If he died, then his estate would pay *Hughes* ten thousand dollars.

Before the details of the wager could be worked out, Al

Stunts in the Sky

Wilson agreed to do the stunt for twenty-five hundred dollars. A mechanic named Phil Jones was to ride in the plane's cabin. Jones's job was to set off a series of smoke pots to give the impression the plane was on fire as it went into its dive.

On the day of the stunt, Wilson took the Gotha to seven thousand feet, leveled off, and pulled the big ship into a stall. Just as the plane nosed over and started earthward, observers on the ground were startled to see a parachute open and float down. No one was supposed to leave the plane until it was much closer to the ground. The parachutist was Al Wilson.

Meanwhile, Phil Jones was busy with his smoke pots, unaware that Wilson had left the ship. Down the plane spun, slamming into the earth to burst into flames, killing Jones instantly.

Afterward, Wilson said he had heard a wing strut snap as he nosed the plane over and had signaled a warning to Jones before his premature departure. But the other pilots were angered by what Wilson had done, and all but a handful refused to work on any film for which he was hired. Wilson died in 1932 in an air-show crash.

Hughes spent more than a million dollars on the flying sequences of *Hell's Angels*. There was a zeppelin raid, an attack on an ammunition dump, and thrilling battles in the sky. But the film was never as successful as *Wings*, neither artistically nor financially.

The deaths that occurred during the production of the film shook Hollywood to its foundations. An article in *Photoplay* concerning the film was titled, "Four Million Deaths and Four Men's Lives." (Stunt people accounted for three of the deaths; the fourth was a cameraman who died of natural causes.)

If the production of *Hell's Angels* did not underscore the deadly nature of stunt flying, an accident that took place in January 1930 certainly did. Twentieth-Century Fox was filming a scene for *Such Men Are Dangerous,* which was based on the death of a noted financier on a mystery-cloaked airplane flight. Three cabin planes took off from Clover Field in Los Angeles with instructions to fly out over the ocean. Riding in the lead plane, piloted by Roscoe Turner, were Warner Baxter, the star of the film, and his "double." The other two planes carried the director, Kenneth Hawks, and nine members of the film's crew.

Turner put his plane on a direct course for Point Firman, where the three planes were to rendezvous and filming was to begin. Suddenly Turner heard someone in the cabin shout out, "Look, they've hit each other!" Turner veered the plane around to get a look. What he saw horrified him. The two planes were tangled together, both afire and falling fast toward the water. Just as they were about to hit, Turner saw the men either fall or jump from the burning mass of metal. He saw the bodies splash into the sea a short distance away from the point where the wreckage struck the water. No one survived.

After that, no producer or actor wanted to be involved in a flying film. *The Dawn Patrol,* which was in production at the time, starred Richard Barthelmess, who absolutely refused to go up in the air. For aerial scenes, Barthelmess sat in a Jenny that was suspended from the roof of a huge sound stage by long cables.

Stunt flying in the 1920s was dominated by Dick Grace,

who, miraculously, lived to die in bed. The 1930s saw the beginning of the Paul Mantz era. Mantz, born in 1903, grew up in Redwood City, California. He was adventurous as a boy and interested in anything mechanical. Airplanes fascinated him. In 1927, the year that Charles Lindbergh became the first to make a solo transatlantic flight, Mantz joined the Air Corps.

After he had been discharged, Mantz arrived in Hollywood, seeking work as a stunt pilot. No one would hire him because he was not a member of the newly formed Motion Picture Pilots Association. A stunt flier could not work in Hollywood unless he was a member of the MPAA. But whenever Mantz applied for membership, he was rejected.

Finally, Mantz got his chance. The MPAA welcomed him as a member and he was assigned to do a stunt for *The Galloping Ghost,* a 1931 film. Mantz was very pleased. But he was also puzzled by his sudden good luck.

The stunt he was to perform seemed to be a simple one. All Mantz had to do was fly an old Steerman biplane past the cameras while the stuntman Bob Rose clung to the upper wing.

As Mantz was completing the low-level pass, he suddenly realized why he had gotten the job. A huge tree loomed up ahead of him, and when he tried to bank to avoid it, the plane would not respond. Rose's body, which lay across the trailing edge of the wing, was jamming the control system. But Mantz knew what to do. He shoved the stick forward, pushing the plane's nose down. The plane slammed into the ground and *bounced* over the tree.

Paul Mantz was Hollywood's leading stunt flier of the 1940s.
(*Hollywood Stuntmen's Hall of Fame*)

For the film *Air Mail,* Mantz coolly flew his Steerman through the open doors of a hangar and out the other side, another stunt that other members of the MPAA refused to do.

It wasn't long before Mantz was Hollywood's top stunt flier. He also became one of the film capital's better-

Stunts in the Sky

known personalities. He was an adviser to Amelia Earhart, one of the most famous female aviators of all time, on her long-distance flights. He established a flying service called the "Honeymoon Express," which transported Hollywood stars to Reno, Nevada for quick weddings.

He founded his own company, United Flight Services, and in time most of the MPAA pilots went to work for it. But Mantz's pilots were never highly paid. Their basic fee was 50 dollars a day, with an additional 250 dollars for a full week of work. No matter who did the flying, Mantz received 250 dollars weekly as "aerial director." Mantz himself performed all the special stunts, for which he negotiated his own fees.

In 1938, Mantz was put in complete charge of the air squadron and pilots for the production of *Men With Wings*, Hollywood's first technicolor air epic and the biggest aerial film since *Hell's Angels*.

When the Japanese bombed Pearl Harbor on December 7, 1941, plunging the United States into World War II, it put an end to stunt flying. The entire Pacific coast was declared a defense zone, and planes were not allowed to go aloft without prior approval from the War Department.

Mantz became Lt. Col. Mantz, commander of the Air Corps's first motion picture unit. One of his responsibilities was to produce government training films to be used to instruct Air Corps cadets in the basic techniques of flying. In these, Mantz often played the role of the feather-brained pilot, diving beneath bridges or through barns, flying upside down and over busy highways, doing all the things cadets were *never* to do.

5

More Stunts in the Sky

In 1950, Darryl Zanuck, one of Hollywood's most noted producers, gave Paul Mantz what was perhaps his toughest assignment. For the film *Twelve O'Clock High,* Mantz, doubling for Gregory Peck, was to crash-land a B-17 bomber in front of the cameras, skidding the plane for almost a quarter of a mile, and ending the sequence by plowing into a tent city. Mantz was to be well paid, receiving six thousand dollars, a stunt record at the time.

Nicknamed "The Flying Fortress," the four-engined B-17 was a great hulk of a plane. The man at the controls needed plenty of help from the copilot to be able to land the aircraft, with the two men having to handle the landing gear, flaps, throttles, mixture controls, cowl flaps, and the radio as the plane came in.

But Mantz was not going to have a copilot. He was going to have to do the stunt alone.

More Stunts in the Sky

Mantz's mechanic, Paul King, welded a steel rod across the four throttle levers so that Mantz could yank them forward or back all at once. The landing gear was no problem, because the script called for it to remain in an "up" position for the scene.

When the day of the stunt arrived, Mantz's chief worry was a stout iron post that had been erected inside one of the tents. Mantz was to slam one wing into the post, which was supposed to spin the plane around. That, Mantz knew, was going to be tricky.

The post was not a big problem—the wind was. As the huge plane lumbered in at the far end of the field, Mantz began having trouble with the controls. When he cut the power, things got worse. Because of a stiff tail wind, he could not get the rudder to respond. It was like trying to steer a speeding automobile over an icy pond.

As he bellied in, Mantz realized that he was going to have to control the plane with the brakes. As gently as possible, he eased the left brake pedal forward with the toe of one boot. When the brake grabbed, it sent the ship into a sudden swerve to the left and toward a line of parked B-17s. Disaster loomed. With his other foot, Mantz quickly jammed on the right brake. The plane slowly straightened out and began its long, grinding, crunching slide into the massed tents.

Mantz braced himself for the collision with the big post. But the plane's momentum was so great that it sliced the post in two as if it were a tent pole. The top half flipped into the air and came sailing right for the cockpit. Mantz ducked. The pole flew over his head and sliced into the canopy. Mantz wasn't even scratched.

Filming of *Flight of the Phoenix* brought death to stunt flier Paul Mantz. *(Movie Star News)*

Mantz's crash landing of the giant B-17 in *Twelve O'Clock High* ranks as one of the most spectacular stunt-flying sequences ever filmed. In 1976, when the motion picture *Midway* was made, the entire crash sequence was used again, a tribute to Mantz, his skill, and his boldness.

To some stuntmen, the lure of "just one more" has proved fatal. Mantz is a case in point. He died in 1965 making *The Flight of the Phoenix,* a film about a surplus cargo plane that crashes in the Sahara desert and is rebuilt and flown to safety by the survivors.

Mantz was sixty-two at the time. The plane he had to fly was a cumbersome freak, its undercarriage resembling a pair of heavy skis. The flight was made under the scorching sun at Butterfly Valley, not far from Yuma, Arizona. The first time he flew the plane, Mantz managed to get it into the air, fly it successfully, and ease it back onto the soft sand without any problems.

On his second try, Mantz's long string of good luck ran out. Riding in the cockpit behind Mantz was Bob Rose, the veteran stuntman who had flown with him in his very first film, *The Galloping Ghost,* in 1931. As Mantz brought the plane in, the skis, instead of gliding over the sand as they had done on his first flight, dug into the ground, causing the plane to flip end over end. The engine broke loose, shot back, and almost tore Mantz's head off. Rose jumped clear and survived with a broken shoulder.

Mantz was remembered in a unique way. *The Flight of the Phoenix* was dedicated to him, and he received special mention in the film's credits. This was in sharp contrast to what had been done in the past, when efforts were made to hush up stuntmen's deaths.

A few years before his death, Mantz had teamed up with tall, slim, forty-two-year-old Frank Tallman, a highly skilled pilot, whose aerial stunts had been featured in such films as *Lafayette Escadrille, Wake Me When It's Over,* and *Twilight Zone.* In 1963, for *It's a Mad Mad Mad Mad World,* Tallman had punched a two-engine Beechcraft through a Styrofoam-and-balsa wood billboard. He made his exit with Styrofoam and balsa wood clogging one engine and a few dents in the wings—and a reputation for being very gutsy. It was not a reputation he tried to cultivate. Indeed, he liked to be known not as a stunt pilot but as a "precision flier."

Frank Tallman pilots a two-engine Beechcraft through a Styrofoam and balsa billboard. *(Hollywood Stuntmen's Hall of Fame)*

Tallman had started flying as a boy of ten, sitting in his father's lap in an old Jenny. He soloed when he was sixteen, served as a flight instructor in the Navy during World War II, and began performing aerial stunts after the war ended and he was discharged. "I never refused to do a stunt," he once told an interviewer. "But there were times I was able to provide a substitute proposal for a stunt that would work better than the original, and would not contain the same risks."

When Tallman and Mantz joined forces, they combined their fleets of planes, hangar space, and names to form the Tallmantz Aviation Company. The merger also produced the Movieland of the Air Museum at the Orange County

More Stunts in the Sky

Airport, at Santa Ana, California, where visitors could view almost fifty antique aircraft.

For well over a decade, Tallman reigned as the film industry's No. 1 stunt pilot—or "precision flier." He gathered and organized more than twenty B-25 bombers for *Catch 22*. His stunts in that film included cutting a dummy in half with the propeller of a B-25. In *The Adversaries*, Tallman lost both wings by crashing through a wooden shack. Tallman also performed the stunts for the television series "Black Sheep Squadron," based on the exploits of the World War II flying ace Pappy Boyington.

In *Charley Varrick*, produced in 1972, Tallman doubled for Walter Matthau, who played the role of a former stunt pilot who had turned to crop dusting to earn a living. When big companies forced Varrick out of the dusting business, he became a bank robber, using aerial acrobatics performed in an old Steerman to make his getaways. That, of course, was where Tallman came in.

Tallman's greatest fun was in reviving the barnstorming era with the director George Roy Hill and Robert Redford for the 1974 film *The Great Waldo Pepper*. The principal planes required for the production were two old Jennies and two Standards. These were among the planes that had been available by the hundreds after World War I, but by the 1970s they had become rare antiques.

Tallman and the producers managed to acquire a Jenny and two Standards, but the second Jenny and a Sopworth Camel had to be built from scratch. Skilled craftsmen were employed to do the work, which took nearly a year.

In one of the film's major stunt sequences, the Great

Tallman succeeded Paul Mantz as Hollywood's No. 1 stunt flier.
(*Hollywood Stuntmen's Hall of Fame*)

Waldo, played by Redford, is to make a transfer from a fast-moving car to a rope ladder suspended from a plane, ascend the ladder to walk about on the wing, and then descend again. That isn't all. The script calls for him to be concentrating so completely on the ladder as he performs the stunt that he fails to see a barn that's dead ahead. The inevitable happens—Waldo smashes into the barn.

Of course, Robert Redford was not going to slam into the barn. A dummy, dressed to look like Redford, would.

Nor was Redford going to climb up the ladder for a bit of wing walking (not in this sequence, anyway; in other scenes, however, Redford did climb out on the wing of an aircraft in flight). A stuntman would substitute for him.

It was a complex stunt, with many hazards involved. One of Tallman's chief worries was that the rope ladder would get snagged when the dummy hit the barn and drag the plane into the ground. This problem was solved by designing a breakaway ladder, which was to pull apart when the dummy smacked into the barn roof.

After thoroughly testing the 1925 Lincoln and the Standard that were to be used in the sequence and making several alterations in each, the cast and crew were ready to begin actual filming runs. Arrangements had been made to use an abandoned field near San Antonio, Texas.

Tallman, at the controls of the Standard, got the speed of the plane equal to that of the fast-moving Lincoln, then brought the bottom rung of the swinging ladder to within exactly three feet of the ground. It took a deft touch, for even the slightest movement of the controls could start the ladder swinging crazily, even though it had been heavily weighted. A camera car, speeding along just ahead of the Lincoln, filmed the action.

Once Tallman had the plane in position, Redford, seated in the front seat of the Lincoln next to the driver, was to hang out of the speeding car and reach for the ladder. This part of the stunt worried Tallman. On a practice run, the heavy ladder had smashed the windshield of the Lincoln, just missing Redford and the driver. Tallman had to handle the controls as gently as possible to minimize the ladder's swing.

More Stunts in the Sky

The sequence went off without any hitches. Then it had to be repeated, the second time with the stuntman John Kazian riding in Redford's place in the Lincoln. Kazian, wearing a rubber mask of Redford's face, was to make the actual transfer from the car to the plane. In the final film, the footage of Redford grabbing the ladder and the sequence of Kazian making the actual ladder ascent would be spliced together, giving the impression that the action was being performed by one person.

Again Tallman got the Standard in position over the speeding Lincoln, and peering down, saw Kazian get a solid grip on the ladder. He eased the plane up and watched as Kazian got his feet on the ladder's bottom rung. Then Tallman flew the plane slowly around the field as Kazian cautiously made his way up the ladder to the wing.

When Kazian got up onto the wing, and Tallman looked out at him, it gave him a jolt. Even though he had seen the stuntman wearing Redford's face mask several times, he still had the feeling it was the real Redford out there.

The final segment of the stunt, in which the dummy on the ladder was to crash into the barn, presented some special problems. The dummy had to be lowered slowly on the rope ladder. To help out in this scene, Tallman called on Scott Newman, the son of the actor Paul Newman and an experienced parachutist. Newman was to ride in the front seat of the Standard and lower the dummy carefully, controlling its arms and legs with ropes as if it were a puppet. Scott had to hang out of the front seat to do it. Once the dummy was in position at the bottom of the ladder, Scott had to make his exit. Otherwise, he'd appear in the film.

More Stunts in the Sky

"Go, Scott!" Tallman shouted out. Scott climbed out onto the wing and fell away. Seconds later his chute opened and Tallman watched as he floated to earth, landing safely near the barn.

Hardly had Scott landed when Tallman's radio crackled. The director was calling, instructing Tallman to make a pass to be sure the camera placement was right.

The second time around the cameras were rolling. Heading in at a speed of about seventy-five miles per hour, Tallman leveled off so that the dummy was about ten feet above the ground. He pulled the plane's nose up slightly as the barn appeared ahead, just clearing the peak of the roof. He heard a tremendous thump and felt the impact as the ladder and the dummy knifed through the breakaway roof. As Tallman turned and climbed, he looked back to see the dummy smash through the rear part of the barn and tumble to a tangled landing in the tall grass behind the structure. Tallman grinned. It couldn't have been better.

Several weeks later, when Tallman was test-flying a 1918 Nieuport 28 that he had rented for the film, misfortune struck. The flight had been uneventful and the plane was handling well, but as he was coming in for his landing, the ship snapped violently into a diving turn to the right. When Tallman went to put his foot on the left rudder pedal to straighten out the plane, he couldn't find any pedal. He ducked his head down and looked for it. His heart sank. The pedal and the post to support it were completely gone.

Now the plane was out of control, spinning dizzily, the ground rushing up to meet him. "I don't think I'm going to

An airplane stunt from *The Great Waldo Pepper* reenacts the dangers of early flight.   (*Movie Star News*)

get out of this alive," Tallman thought to himself. But he did not panic. His hands raced over the instrument panel, getting all the switches off to lessen the chance of a fire on impact. Then he threw one arm in front of his face and braced himself—and waited.

Ten minutes later he awakened to find himself looking down at the floor of the misshapen cockpit. Blood was running from a big gash in his head and trickling into his shoes. There was no great pain, only a drowsy feeling. He could hear birds singing and crickets chirping. It was like a weird dream.

The Nieuport 28 had slammed into high tension wires, which had stopped the plane dead in midair, and the impact had knocked Tallman unconscious. Then the plane had dropped straight down about seventy feet onto a riverbank where it now rested.

Tallman was struggling to get out of the cockpit when help arrived. A nurse stopped the bleeding and a helicopter was summoned to airlift him to the hospital.

Tallman's injuries didn't concern him as much as what had caused the accident. He instructed a mechanic to locate the broken rudder pedal. He knew that if it had been structural failure that had caused the crash, investigators would want to see the faulty part.

At the hospital, doctors found that Tallman had broken two vertabrae and a rib and had torn some muscles. But he shrugged off the injuries. "It was a small price to pay for staying alive," he said. Three weeks later he was out of the hospital and back flying.

One other sequence in *The Great Waldo Pepper* should be mentioned. Tallman, flying a Standard, swooped down on a small town (Elgin, Texas, actually), then skimmed the plane above the pavement of the main street. There was less than three feet of space between the plane's wing tips and the buildings. In addition, Tallman had to be on the lookout for crosscurrents at street intersections, pedestrians who ignored orders to stay in doorways, and people who craned their necks from upper-story windows to see what was going on.

Of all the films that Tallman worked on, *The Great Waldo Pepper* was his favorite. He felt a sense of regret when he had finished work on the picture. "I don't think we'll have so much fun again," he said.

When *The Great Waldo Pepper* was released, reviewers hailed the movie's stunt-flying sequences. *The New York Times* declared that the "spectacular aerial sequences... are as good as anything you've probably ever seen about the early days of flying."

In April 1978, Tallman flew north to San Francisco to scout locations for a new movie on which he expected to work. On his return home, his plane, a twin-engine Piper Aztec, crash-landed amidst the rugged terrain of the Cleveland National Forest not far from his destination, the Orange County Airport. Tallman died in the crash. Officials speculated that the heavy storms that occurred that night were probably a factor.

Movies and television shows about flying can be made without ever leaving the studio. Actors can be strapped into fake cockpits that can be turned every which way. Models instead of real planes can be used. The results are usually terrible.

When a director wanted to depict a real plane doing real stunts, he sought out Frank Tallman—or Paul Mantz, Dick Grace, Omar Locklear, or any one of a handful of others. They would fly no matter how risky the stunt. It's too early to tell, but with Frank Tallman's death, their term may have ended.

6

Cars as Stars

The airplane's Hollywood heyday occurred during the late 1920s and early 1930s, as typified by films such as *Wings*. With automobiles—and automobile chases and crashes—it's been much different. Cars began to be handed important roles only in recent times, this partly because of two films, *Bullitt* and *The French Connection*. *Bullitt* was released in 1969; *The French Connection,* in 1971. Both were seen frequently on television during the 1970s. The car chases in these two films, as action sequences, have been compared with the best in movie history.

Today, films and television are more deeply involved with cars than ever before. Cars are seen rocketing along freeways at bullet speeds, careening through city traffic, plummeting off piers and high cliffs, tumbling down hillsides, spinning, skidding, turning over, crashing, exploding, and bursting into flames. Motorcycles and trucks have also gotten into the act.

A car stunt is performed on a New York street for the film *Gloria*.
(*Harry Madsen*)

Of course, car stunts have been included in the movies since the earliest times. The Keystone Kops performed all sorts of antics with their Kop Wagon. Keystone had its very own stunt driver, Del Lord.

But the kinds of stunts one sees today weren't possible then. The cars simply couldn't generate the speed necessary to execute them.

When a spectacular stunt did happen to be performed, it was considered an important event. In 1916, California spring floods washed out a highway bridge that crossed a stream near the town of Camarillo. Filmmakers set up cameras at the washout. With Thomas Chatterton at the wheel, they sent a car hurtling over the thirty-five-foot gap between bridge sections. The sequence was used in a film titled *The Secret of the Submarine,* released the same year. Chatterton's feat was considered of such significance that local schoolchildren were dismissed for the day so they could witness the thrill-making.

Safety precautions taken by early stunt drivers were primitive when compared with those used today. William Duncan prepared for a ramp jump in a 1922 serial by rolling up his overcoat and wedging it between the steering wheel and his chest.

Cliff Bergere, a well-known stuntman of the 1920s and 1930s and surely the best stunt driver of the period, pioneered in the use of many automobile safety devices. A one-time professional race driver, Bergere often spoke out about the danger of employing amateur drivers—or "wildcats," as he called them—to perform car stunts.

Not only was it dangerous; it was costly. Bergere once received an offer to drive and wreck a Ford coupe by piling it into the front end of a trolley car. Bergere asked for five hundred dollars to do the "gag." The director said he couldn't afford to pay that much and hired an amateur at five dollars a day.

"He was sorry later," Bergere said. "The wildcat tried it fourteen times, wrecking fourteen Fords. They worked days before they got the right shot. There was no economy in that."

"An experienced man knows all the tricks," said Bergere. "To turn over an automobile, you have to know just how to rig your machine in advance. You take out the driver's seat so you can sit lower. You saw off the gearshift handle and the hand brake so you'll have more room to lie down as the car spins over and over. You have to remove the door handles and pad your car inside so you won't get bruised too badly, and put in safety belts, such as are used in airplanes, where you think you will need them. These prevent you from being thrown around as the car whips over.

"Then, across the front part of the body, beginning just below the hood, you fasten a strip of angle iron that's about one inch thick and two inches wide, and you run it right around the car. You do the same in the back. It makes a cradle for you.

"Then you take all but half a gallon of gas from the tank so the car won't catch fire. You run the car up to about forty miles an hour, turn it over, and let nature take its course."

In the filming of an important crash scene in *Twelve Crowded Hours* in 1939, Bergere took these and other precautions. A huge truck operated by gangsters, traveling at a high speed, was to bear down on a taxicab. The panic-stricken cab driver was to swerve to his left, whereupon the truck was to smash into the smaller vehicle, turn it over, and ram it up against a building. Bergere was to drive the cab.

The shock absorbers were removed from the cab to make it turn over easily. The brakes on the right wheels were disconnected to assure that when the taxi swerved, it would swerve to the left.

On the first few tries, the driver of the truck decided that the crash was unsafe and swerved off to one side. On the sixth try, the two vehicles collided as planned, the big truck shoving the taxi more than thirty feet before it slammed it into the building. The cab was so completely demolished that it seemed that no one inside could possibly be alive. The sequence called for dozens of extras to swarm around the battered vehicle while the cameras continued to grind away, and this added to the anxiety of the moment. But there was really no cause for concern. As soon as the director called out, "Cut!," Bergere stepped out uninjured.

He received 350 dollars for the stunt. The cab was hauled off to the junkyard.

In the mid-1930s, according to Bergere, there were only seven men in the stunting profession capable of doing spectacular car stunts. One of these was Carey Loftin, who later was to design some of Hollywood's most elaborate action scenes involving cars. From Mississippi, Loftin began working in motion pictures in 1936. Before that, he had been a road-show stunt driver for several years. Road-show drivers were something like aerial barnstormers, except that they performed in cars or on motorcycles at small-town tracks. While Carey's specialty was motorcycle work, he also crashed cars, drove them on two wheels, and jumped them between ramps.

At Paramount Pictures, Carey was assigned to do a motorcycle stunt in which the cycle and a taxicab were to almost collide head on at an intersection. The script called for the motorcycle to spin a full 360 degrees as Carey slammed on the brakes.

The director explained to Carey that they were going to

Carey Loftin doubled for Kane Richmond in *Spy Smasher*, a serial.
(*Hollywood Stuntmen's Hall of Fame*)

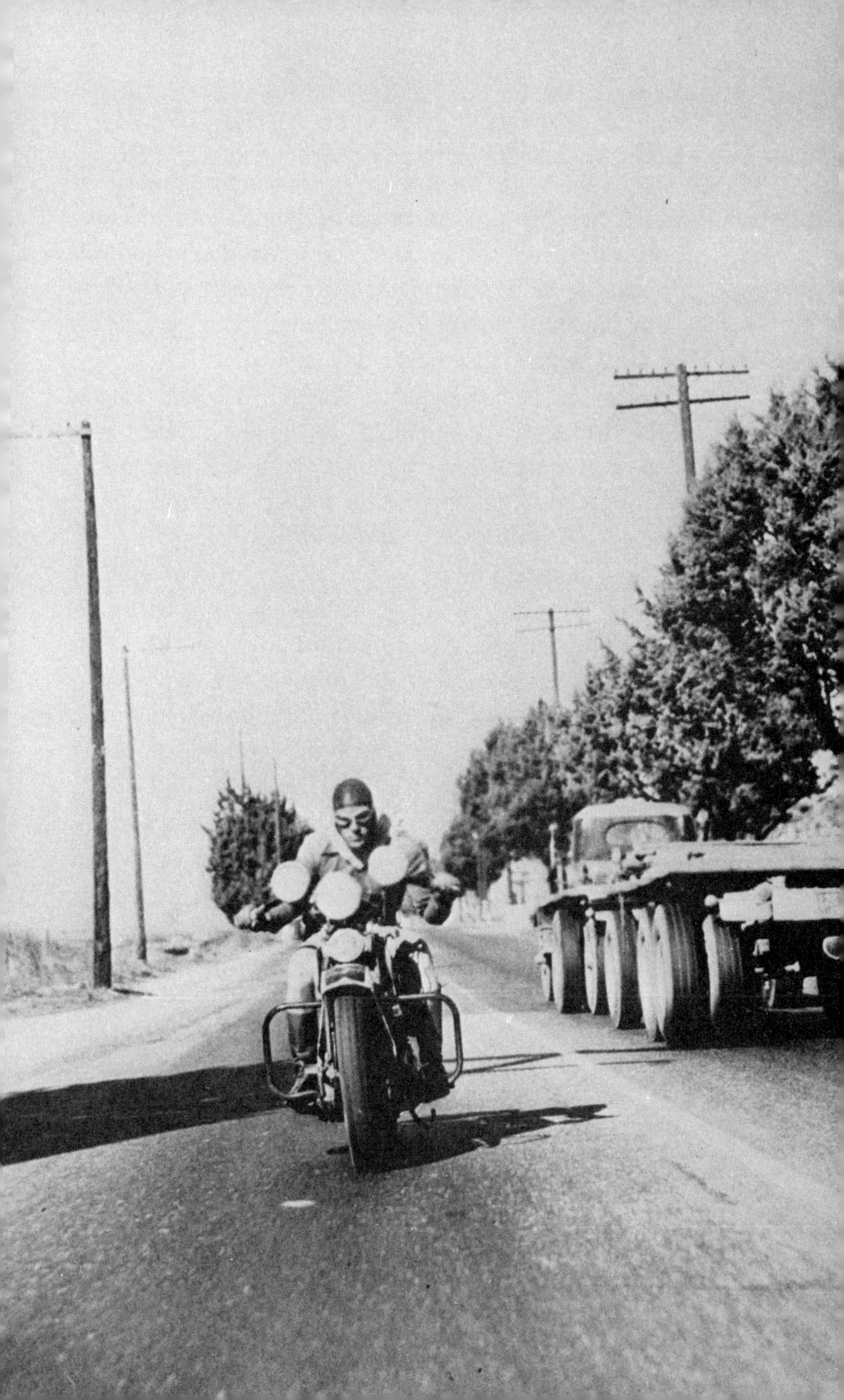

do the scene in three different stages. First, there would be a long shot of the motorcycle as it barreled toward the intersection. Next, there would be a long shot of the taxi. Last, a turntable would be put down and the motorcycle mounted upon it. After Carey had seated himself on the cycle, the turntable would be revolved, giving the effect of the spinning stop that the director wanted.

Loftin laughed when he heard this. "You don't have to build all that stuff," he said. "I can *do* that." Whereupon he revved up the motorcycle, brought it screaming toward the intersection, jammed on the brakes, and spun it *three* times.

The technician who was in charge of the turntable scowled and accused Carey of showing off. "That's just what I did, showed off," Loftin was to say in later years. "But it sure helped me to get work at Paramount."

During the 1940s, Carey drove in countless motorcyle and car chases, sometimes with the emphasis on thrills, other times on comedy. He worked with W.C. Fields in *The Bank Dick* and on many of the Abbott and Costello comedies.

Sometimes Loftin would "chase himself." Suppose the sequence was to show a motorcycle in pursuit of a car. The scene would be shot twice. The first time, Loftin would be at the wheel of the car and another stuntman would drive the motorcycle. Loftin, as the driver of the car, would take all kinds of hair-raising chances. Then Loftin and the other stunt driver would reverse roles, and Carey would pilot the motorcycle through a series of wild maneuvers. When the film was edited, Loftin's driving sequences would be spliced together. As the audiences finally saw it, Loftin would, in fact, be pursuing Loftin.

In a film that Loftin worked on with W.C. Fields, a cop on a motorcycle chases a limousine, with the motorcycle piling into a ditch filled with workmen. In the film's final version, Loftin is the man at the wheel of the car and he drives the motorcycle—and he also plays one of the men in the ditch. "You could do things like that when the assistant director was a friend of yours," said Loftin.

It was Carey Loftin who supervised the wrecking crew of three stuntmen, including himself, and the fourteen leading sports-car drivers, most of them veterans of Grand Prix competition, for what was called "the last auto race in the world" in the film *On the Beach,* produced by Stanley Kramer in 1959. Because all the drivers were doomed to die because of radioactive fallout, they piloted their cars without the slightest regard for danger to life or limb.

The Riverside Raceway, about sixty miles east of Los Angeles, was where the action was filmed. It took six weeks. Seven cameras photographed the action. Before shooting was finished, three cameras were destroyed in separate accidents. Two were struck by cars. A third, placed on the rear of a racing car, tore loose from its mounting during a spin.

A camera in a helicopter was supposed to shoot the race scenes from above. Because the helicopter had a top speed of "only" 90 miles per hour, it could not keep pace with the racing cars, which tore along at speeds of up to 170 miles per hour. The camera car also had trouble keeping up with the pack. A powerful but aged Cadillac, it couldn't go

Cars as Stars

much faster than 80 miles per hour. For many shots, cameras had to be mounted on race cars.

Loftin hired two friends, Harvey Perry and Dale Van Sickle, to assist him with the driving. They spun and skidded their race cars, jammed the pack, scraped guardrails at wide-open speed, climbed banks, rolled over, bounced end-over-end, hurtled into the air, collided, caught fire, and blew up. Of course, any car that burned or exploded had a dummy at the wheel.

The stuntmen and professional drivers were so close to the action that sometimes their clothing was scorched or they were struck by parts and debris. Only two injuries,

This fiery car stunt in *On the Beach* has become a film classic.
(*Movie Star News*)

both minor, were sustained. Rocketing out of a turn at seventy miles per hour, Perry sideswiped Van Sickle's car, and both of them rolled over and over. Perry, a longtime stunt driver, managed to escape with a sprained neck. Van Sickle, a one-time All-American football player, cut his forehead. Both were back driving in less than half an hour.

Loftin, exposing himself to about as much danger as any race course can offer, came out of the action unhurt. But on the evening he arrived home after the last day of filming, he reached to get his suitcase of the back of his car and sprained his knee.

Loftin's most famous job was the car-chase sequence in *Bullitt*. It was such an outstanding piece of work that it became an industry standard. "I want a *Bullitt*-type chase," producers would say.

The film's story concerns a bright, tough, charming San Francisco police lieutenant, played by Steve McQueen, who becomes involved in a gangland plot that leaves a dead witness on his hands. He has only a few days to solve the case before a politically ambitious district attorney demotes him. Driving his Ford Mustang through the streets of San Francisco, he spots a Dodge Charger containing the gunmen who had been imported to commit the murder. He gives chase, creating the focal point of the film, a twelve-minute sequence over and around San Francisco's roller-coaster hills with the cars reaching speeds of one hundred miles per hour.

It was usual for chases to be shot by second-unit directors at locations outside the studio. They would film moving cars and the crashes—all the action.

Cars as Stars

Later the star would be inserted into the scene by using a process called rear-screen projection. The star would be photographed while seated behind the wheel of a car shell bolted to the floor of the sound stage. The camera would focus on his face as the footage shot by the second unit was projected on a screen behind the car. The resulting "process shot," as it was called, if photographed carefully, could fool just about everyone in the audience.

In *Bullitt,* however, there was to be no rear-screen projection, no trick photography. It was to be shot entirely on location, with Loftin acting as stunt coordinator.

One reason that Loftin was able to lay out the whole chase scene on the streets of San Francisco was that Steve McQueen, an accomplished driver, agreed to do the actual chase driving in the Mustang. The stuntman Bill Hickman was to be at the wheel of the Charger.

Both automobiles had to be partially rebuilt for the film. Two steel sections were mounted on each side of the Mustang near the rear springs. In some scenes, the Mustang was to race uphill so fast that it was to be rocketed into the air at the top. The steel reinforcing was to prevent the car from caving in as it landed back down. Big, wide wheels and tires and stronger springs and shock absorbers were installed on both cars.

To be able to get the action on film, a special car had to be designed that could keep up with the Mustang and Charger. This car, which came to be known as a "Bullittmobile," consisted of a souped-up Chevrolet that instead of a front bumper had a platform that was big enough to hold a camera and a cameraman.

A camera was also mounted on the Mustang and operated from inside the car. This camera gave the audience the feeling of what it was like to see through the windshield of a car that was leaping, bouncing, and spinning at breakneck speeds. Loftin rehearsed the driving and split-second timing in slow motion first, working up to the speed at which the cars were to be driven during the filming.

The chase, which lasts twelve minutes in the movie's final version, took two weeks to film. The director Peter Yates had some new ideas about what he wanted to show on film. "It's more exciting to show a succession of near misses," he said, "than a costly series of collisions." As the vehicles spun on turns or flattened on impact, Yates's cameras often concentrated on the flexing of car tires, burning rubber, or flying sparks. Yates showed the way the hands of a driver skillfully handled the steering wheel, and he let the audience hear the screech of tires and the surge of powerful engines.

McQueen impressed everyone with his driving skill. One day, close-ups of McQueen were to be photographed as he drove the car at full throttle. The camera was mounted to the hood of the car and directed toward McQueen through the windshield. Yates was on the backseat floor, where he operated the camera by remote control.

McQueen gunned the car to life, and they started out. Faster and faster the car went. As they started down a long hill, Yates looked at the speedometer. It read 120 miles an hour. Then he checked the camera and saw it was out of film. He tapped McQueen on the shoulder. "Slow down!" he said. "We've got to stop and reload."

Cars as Stars

The car did not slow down. McQueen shouted that there was something wrong with the brakes. Coolly, McQueen began downshifting, changing gears so as to check the car's speed. The engine strained. The gearbox whined. McQueen weaved the car from one side of the road to the other. It began slowing down. By the time he brought the car to a stop on the steep gravel shoulder, both he and Yates were laughing heartily. But later Yates was to say, "McQueen's proficiency at the wheel... is something I'm thankful for; his driving may have saved my life."

After the hillside scenes, another sequence took place on a long stretch of open freeway, which, of course, was closed by the police during the filming. Oncoming cars seen in the film were driven by stuntmen.

The scene called for McQueen and Hickman to drive at exceptionally high speeds side by side. Occasionally, their cars were to slam together as they tried to knock each other off the road. At one point, Hickman thumped into McQueen's car and sideswiped a remote-control camera that was mounted on it. "If there had been a cameraman behind the lens, he would have been wiped out," McQueen said afterward.

The chase ends when the pursued car crashes into a gasoline station and the killers meet flaming death in the explosion of scores of gasoline drums. For this, Loftin used the knowledge and experience he had gained in a similar crash staged during the filming of *On the Beach*.

The car that was to crash was driverless and fitted with special switches that would make it explode on cue. To control the vehicle, Loftin attached his own car to it by means of a heavy steel towing bar which he could release from his seat. With the cars locked together, Loftin sped down a specially laid-out course, pressed the button that released the crash car, and then floored the accelerator of his own car to speed out of the shot.

The director William Friedkin once said that *Bullitt* offered " . . . what was probably the best car chase of the sound film era." When Friedkin agreed to direct *The French Connection* in 1970, he made up his mind " . . . to do another kind of chase, one which, while it might remind the people of *Bullitt,* would not be essentially similar."

Instead of having a car chasing a car, Friedkin hit upon the idea of having Jimmy (Popeye) Doyle, a cop, played by Gene Hackman, commandeer a car to chase a killer trying to escape on a moving elevated subway train. Hackman would have to drive with one eye on the traffic and pedestrians and the other eye on his quarry.

Bill Hickman was to double for Hackman. He was to drive a 1970 Pontiac four-door sedan, equipped with a four-speed shift. The New York City Transit Authority gave Friedkin permission to use a stretch of track in a Brooklyn line running from Coney Island to Manhattan. Filming was done in the winter of 1970–71. It was bitterly cold. Sometimes camera equipment froze. More than once, the elevated train froze and wouldn't start.

The chase involved five major stunts. The first one turned out to be more thrill packed than anyone planned. Hickman was to race the Pontiac beneath the elevated tracks. A second car was to shoot out of an intersection. Hickman was to narrowly miss it, go into a spin, cut across

The French Connection car chase between police and underworld figures led to this parkway pileup. *(Movie Star News)*

a service station driveway, and get back underneath the elevated track. The stunt driver in the second car mistimed his approach, and instead of screeching to a halt a few feet from Hickman's car, slammed into it broadside. Neither man was hurt, but both cars were demolished.

The back-up car had to be called into service for the other stunts. In one of these, Hickman speeds through a red light at an intersection. A woman wheeling a baby steps off the curb into his path. Hickman swerves and crashes into a pile of garbage cans. The woman was a stuntwoman, of course. There was no "real" baby in the carriage.

Another stunt was filmed from the backseat of Hickman's car. He pulls up behind a truck that bears a sign saying, "Drive carefully." As Hickman starts to pass the truck on the left, the driver makes an abrupt left turn. Hickman's car goes into a spin and the truck collides with a second car.

Still another stunt called for Hickman to turn in the "wrong" direction up a one-way street in his desperate pursuit of the train. One near miss after another with oncoming traffic results.

The French Connection won an Academy Award as Best Picture of 1971. Friedkin won the award for Best Director.

How many movie and television automobile chases and crashes were spawned by *The French Connection* and *Bullitt* is anybody's guess. But during the 1970s, they became commonplace.

Television now features almost as many car chases as commercials. "B.A.D. Cats," introduced on ABC-TV in 1979, is typical. The series was described as offering "the fastest action on television, with two young stock-car racing superstars turned Los Angeles cops." It is not difficult to imagine the content of each show.

"It seems like every picture today has something about cars," says Carey Loftin, who then adds, "Thank God." Whether or not it's the result of divine intervention, Carey is busy all the time. He recently staged stunts involving cars for *Hagen*, a 1980 television series, and *High Point*, a Canadian film released the same year.

Auto-racing films have gained favor, too. *Le Mans*,

Cars as Stars

Death Race 2000, and *Bobby Deerfield* were among those offered in the 1970s.

Then there was *Smokey and the Bandit*. This film tells the story of a driver of legendary skill named Bandit, played by Burt Reynolds, who takes a sizable bet to race eighteen hundred miles from Georgia to Texas and back in the space of twenty-eight hours, returning with four hundred cases of beer. His friend drives his tractor-trailer rig, while Bandit takes the wheel of his Pontiac Trans Am, acting as a blocker whenever Smokey ("the Law") turns up. After a few minutes of plot and character development, the film becomes one long chase sequence.

Released in 1977, *Smokey and the Bandit* now ranks as one of the most popular motion pictures of all time, right up there with *Gone With the Wind, Rocky, the Sting,* and other box-office champions. The film's success spawned *Smokey and the Bandit II*, released in 1981. The final

This car melee was part of *Smokey and the Bandit II*.
(Hollywood Stuntmen's Hall of Fame)

Cars as Stars

scene was shot on a dry lake bed in Nevada. It required forty diesel semis, fifty late model Pontiac and Dodge stunt cars, forty stuntmen and five stunt women. In addition, a tow truck, a fire truck, an ambulance, and two hundred seventy-five pieces of motion picture equipment were involved.

The scene's climatic moment came when stuntman Gary Davis raced a stripped down 1979 Plymouth at a speed of 80 miles an hour up a wooden ramp that butted up against the rear end of a double-tiered car carrier, sailed it 163 feet, and smacked it down on the desert floor. He made the shot and broke a record. Stunting had come a long way since Del Lord and the Kop Wagon.

7

"Daredevil Daughters"

Moviegoers of the 1930s and 1940s thought they were seeing Joan Blondell driving an automobile through a fence in *The Perfect Specimen,* Carole Lombard drowning in *True Confession,* Irene Dunne cracking a whip while roller-skating in *Joy of Living,* and Judith Anderson getting pummeled by a murderer in *Pursued*—but they weren't. They were seeing Betty Danko, Mary Wiggins, Loretta Rush, and Audrey Scott, leading stuntwomen of the time. A fan magazine called them "daredevil daughters of celluloid drama."

Betty Danko's specialty was falls. She fell into ditches, lakes, and pools, through trapdoors, from piano tops, over chairs and tables, and down flights of stairs and laundry chutes. She once fell backward from a height of twenty-five feet into a pool containing only thirty-two inches of water—"all for the sake of art and paycheck," she once said.

Up until fairly recent times, men often donned wigs and substituted for women when hazardous stunts were needed. (*Movie Star News*)

Sometimes falling produced unexpected hazards. In *Murder, He Says,* a Paramount film of the late 1930s, Betty Danko and Audrey Scott took part in a chase scene. The script called for them to run through a hayloft and jump out the back door, landing in a pile of hay almost as big as a house, the top of which was almost fifteen feet below the barn door. The hay was to conceal them from their pursuers.

Everything went as planned. The two women raced through the door and plunged down into the soft hay pile.

Down they went, deeper and deeper. It was pitch black inside the hay. Worse, there was hardly any air. Gasping for breath, they began to struggle, looking for a way out. Betty started growing dizzy. Audrey, choking on hay and dust, felt a sharp pain in her side. "We're going to smother to death," she thought to herself.

Then suddenly the two women were in sunlight and breathing again. Workmen had been digging frantically in the hay pile in an effort to find them. The two women crawled out slowly, both wearing expressions of relief.

Betty was once hired by Hal Roach Studios to double for Patsy Kelly in a scene that involved a cougar, or mountain lion. Today, animal training is a special branch of film production, and strict safety measures are observed. This wasn't always the case. Studios used to obtain animals anywhere they could, from circuses, zoos, or random owners. Professional handlers weren't always available. Accidents sometimes occurred as a result.

Betty first met the cougar she was to work with on one of the studio's sound stages. The lion was lying quietly on the floor, its owner nearby. Betty spoke to the big cat, who

"Daredevil Daughters"

looked at her passively. Just as she was beginning to think she was making friends with the animal, the cougar suddenly lashed out with one paw at a brightly beaded moccasin she was wearing. She gasped and pulled back her foot just in time.

Betty was worried. She spoke to the lion's owner and asked him what she should do.

"Put out your foot again," he said. "Put it out where he can see it."

The lion stared at the moccasin and started whisking his tail back and forth.

"Don't be afraid," the owner said. "Put your foot nearer."

Suddenly the animal pounced, clamping Betty's leg between its two front paws, the claws sinking deeply into her flesh. Betty cried out in pain and horror. Then the creature began to tear the leg with its teeth.

"The pain was incredible," Betty was to say later. "Each bite was torture. I wanted to pass out, but I couldn't." While Betty was able to return to work after a hospital stay, her leg was badly scarred.

Many stuntwomen of the time were trained as trick riders in rodeos. They were "cowgirls." Other young women were circus performers, usually aerialists, before they tried stunting. Still others were able to obtain stunt work in films because of their aquatic ability.

Mary Wiggins belonged to the last category. In Tampa, Florida, where she grew up, she won acclaim as a diver for her high school team. Not long after graduation, she was doing spectacular high dives in motion pictures.

That was just the beginning. Mary took up flying,

Mary Wiggins was a champion diver for her high school team before becoming a stuntwoman. *(Hollywood Stuntmen's Hall of Fame)*

earned a pilot's license, and started parachute jumping and wing walking. She also drove motorcycles through fences and crashed and turned over automobiles. Once, on a barnstorming tour that took her into New England, Mary drove a huge locomotive head on into a second locomotive at the Brockton (Massachusetts) Fair, leaping from the engine cab an instant before the collision. She escaped with a broken thumb.

That broken thumb was about the worst injury Mary sustained in a stunting career that lasted for more than a decade. When she did seriously hurt herself, it was when she went swimming for the fun of it. She dived into shallow water, fracturing several vertebrae.

"I'm stunting," Mary once told an interviewer, "first, because it's full of excitement, and I like excitement. Next, because I can make a better living at it than I probably could at anything else."

Loretta Rush was another stuntwoman of the time who used her skill in swimming and diving as a stepping-stone to a career in stunting. Her first film assignment was to dive off a fifty-foot cliff into a stone-quarry pond. She was sixteen years old.

Loretta had several brushes with death during her long career. One of her scariest moments came during the filming of *Flowing Gold,* a silent movie in which she doubled for Anna Q. Nilsson. The stunt involved a flood scene in which a house was to be washed down a stream that was aflame from spilled gasoline. Loretta was to cling to the house's rooftop.

Technicians at Paramount Studios constructed a huge, rectangular tank and filled it with water. A frame house, which they had also built, was then floated in the tank. A tractor out of camera range was to tow the house from one end of the tank to the other, giving the appearance that the structure was being swept along in a fast-moving current.

On the day of the filming, Loretta climbed to the top of

"Daredevil Daughters"

the roof and got into position. The surface of the water was sprayed with gasoline and ignited. The signal was given to the tractor driver, and he revved up the engine. The cameras started grinding.

Suddenly the house began overturning, flinging Loretta toward the fire and water. She plunged to the bottom of the tank. She was smart enough to stay beneath the surface until workmen doused the flames. When she emerged from the tank, she was gasping for air but unhurt.

In a long career as a stuntwoman, Loretta Rush had several brushes with death. *(Hollywood Stuntmen's Hall of Fame)*

Audrey Scott was a skilled rider and champion polo player when she embarked on a career as a stuntwoman. In one of her first assignments, Audrey's lack of experience caused problems. She was to ride a horse along a road at the edge of a wooded area. A speeding car would pass her. Then, after the car had traveled another one hundred feet or so, it would swerve off the road and turn over. The stuntman Floyd Ciswell would be at the wheel. After the crash, the script called for Audrey to ride toward the automobile, but not up to it.

The cameras began to roll. Audrey came into view astride the horse, moving at a gentle trot. In the distance behind, the car approached. Audrey turned her head, just managing to catch a glimpse of it as it sped by. The car swerved abruptly and overturned. The director nodded in approval.

Audrey had never seen a car stunt before. She cried out in horror, certain that a real crash had taken place and the driver was pinned beneath the wreckage. She jumped from her horse and started running toward the overturned car. "Floyd! Floyd!," she called out at the top of her lungs.

The voice of the director, blaring over a loudspeaker, brought her to her senses. "Stop!" he shouted. "Get out of the shot!"

Then Audrey saw Floyd pulling himself out of the wreck. He wasn't even scratched. She realized she had ruined the take and the scene would have to be reshot.

Audrey found even more to worry about when she was assigned to play the role of an ambulance driver in the making of a World War I film at Universal Studios.

Dressed in a khaki blouse and pants, heavy boots, and a jaunty cap, she had to drive the ambulance at top speed over a muddy, heavily rutted road. Before filming began, she made the rough, bouncy drive several times without difficulty.

It was late in the afternoon and only a few minutes of sunlight were left. Once dusk arrived, no more filming would be possible. The director told Audrey to get the ambulance to the starting point as quickly as possible so that filming could begin. He also ordered to prop men to stand by the roadside at the end of the run and hold big aluminum mirrors to reflect the last rays of the sun toward the ambulance.

Audrey got the signal to start the ambulance moving. She built up speed quickly. The ambulance jolted and swayed and she had to struggle to maintain control of the vehicle.

As she neared the end of the run, she suddenly looked up to see that the two men holding the reflectors were standing in the ambulance's path. They were looking at the camera beside them, not at the onrushing vehicle. Audrey wanted to scream, but she couldn't. She grabbed the wheel with both hands and pulled it to the right with all her strength. The ambulance skidded crazily. One of the men dropped his reflector and jumped off the road and right into the front of the skidding ambulance. When he saw his mistake, he jumped back. But as the ambulance swerved by him, there was a sickening thud as the vehicle struck him.

Audrey was thrown from the ambulance as it skidded

and landed face down in the mud. She sobbed, certain that she had killed a man, or almost killed him.

Crew members ran to her. "How bad is he hurt?" she asked, tears streaming down her cheeks.

One of the men shrugged. "He's all right," he said. "Just bruised a little."

Audrey managed to grin. She was rushed back to the studio for a medical checkup. The doctor found no injuries but said that she was suffering from shock. Audrey was quick to agree.

In *Pursued,* Audrey doubled for Judith Anderson in a scene that unfolded inside an old farmhouse constructed within one of the huge sound stages at Warner Brothers. There had been a gunfight in which a man was slain. Dean Jagger, the killer, was dragging the dead man out for burial when Judith Anderson rushed into the room, grabbed Dean by the shoulder, and spun him around. At this point, Judith Anderson made her exit and Audrey took her place. As soon as she was in position, Dean drew back his right hand and slapped Audrey hard across the face. The force of the blow knocked her to her knees. It took several minutes before her head stopped swimming and she could get her jaw working.

The scene had to be repeated. Again Dean's slap knocked Audrey to her knees. This time, as the script directed, she leaped back at him. He grabbed her by the shoulders and shook her violently, and then shoved her away with all his might. Audrey went sprawling.

"Cut!" she heard the director say. Audrey didn't move. She just wanted to lay there for a while and rest.

"*Daredevil Daughters*"

Audrey never got to see the stormy scene on film. Neither did anyone else: When the picture was released the fight scene was cut out. It was considered too violent.

During the 1950s, Helen Thurston was the best known of the Hollywood stuntwomen. Born in 1923, the daughter of a minister, she doubled for Marilyn Monroe, Jane Russell, Betty Grable, and other glamorous stars of the time. Helen did high falls, and she could skid and spin cars. She was also an accomplished swimmer and diver and doubled for Esther Williams, Hollywood's aquatic queen.

Lila Finn, whose career in stunting spanned three decades, established a record for women in 1961, with the fee she received for wrecking a sailboat in the film *A Summer Place*. Lila was doubling for Sandra Dee. On the day the stunt was to be performed, strong winds whipped the waters of the bay. It became so rough that most boats refused to go out. But Lila piled the boat on the rocks, just as she was supposed to do, then swam away unharmed. She was paid fourteen hundred dollars.

Jeannie Epper, Donna Carrett, Julie Johnson, and Kitty O'Neil were among the best-known stuntwomen of the 1970s. Kitty's story is unusual. She was born in Corpus Christi, Texas. Not long after her birth, her father died in an airplane crash. When she was five months old, Kitty fell victim to three diseases at the same time—measles, mumps and smallpox. They left her hearing destroyed.

Kitty's mother was determined that her daughter would lead a normal life despite her handicap. After taking special courses at the University of Texas in how to communi-

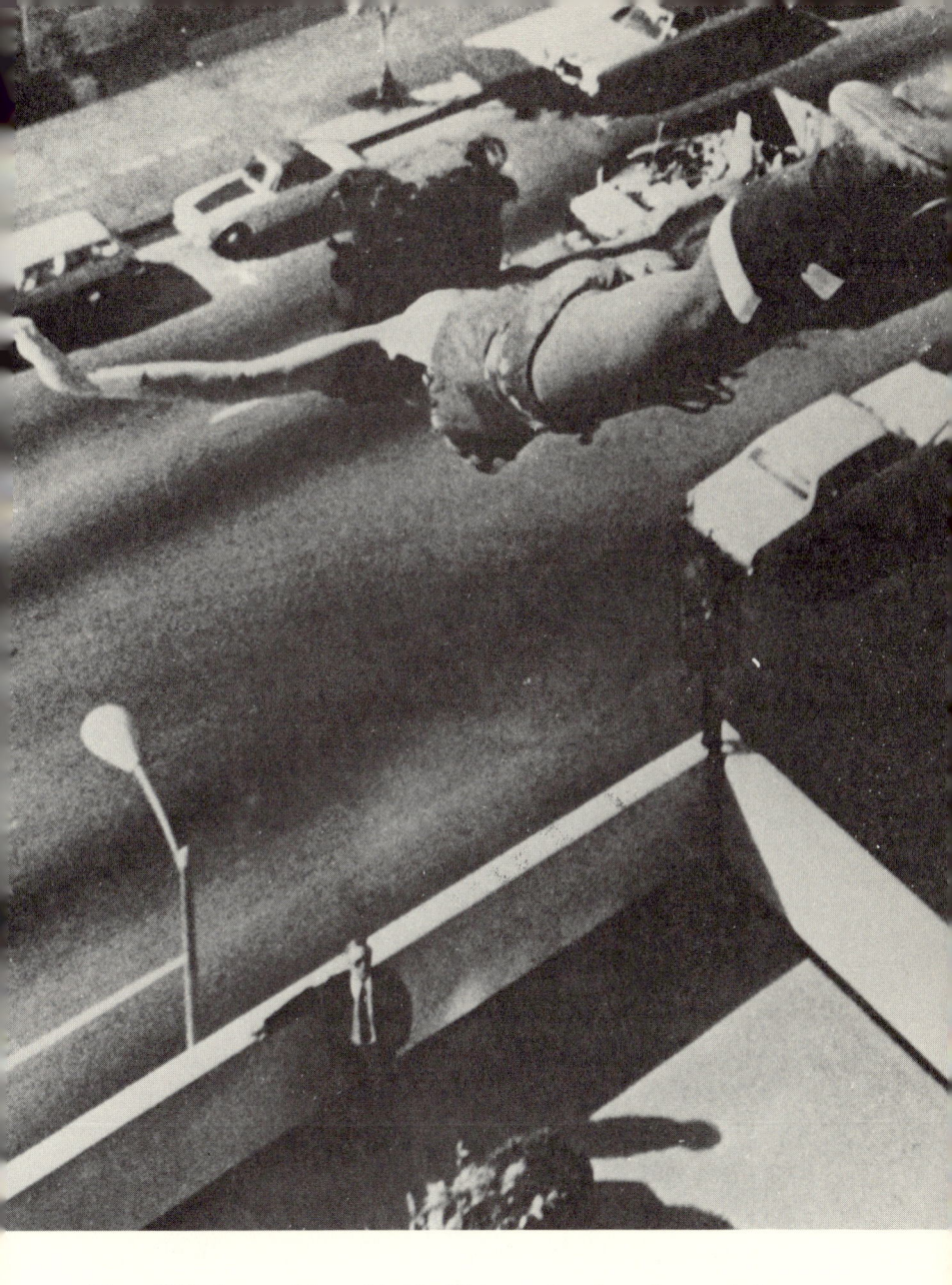

Kitty O'Neil resembles a bird in flight as she dives for an air bag during filming of *Wonder Woman*. *(United Press International)*

cate with deaf people, Mrs. O'Neil taught Kitty how to read lips and speak. Kitty entered the public school system in Wichita Falls, Texas in the third grade. She took piano lessons and learned to play the cello, sensing the different notes by the variations in vibrations the strings produced.

Kitty also learned how to swim. At twelve, she began swimming in competition. At a swimming meet in Oklahoma, one of the team's divers failed to show up. Kitty asked to take her place. She won a first-place gold medal with her dives. After that, she gave up swimming to devote more time to diving. Six months later, Kitty won an AAU Junior Olympics diving championship in Texas.

When she was sixteen Kitty moved to Anaheim, California to attend the diving school operated by Dr. Sammy Lee, an Olympic gold medalist in 1948 and 1952. Dr. Lee couldn't rely on his usual method of shouting instructional advice, telling Kitty when to twist or tuck in her dive. Instead, he used a pistol loaded with blanks. Kitty would feel the shock waves when the gun was fired, and react in midair.

Kitty graduated from Anaheim High School with honors. She was named "Young American of the Month" by *American Youth Magazine*. The article about her said, "Kitty snaps up diving awards like a hungry fish—five trophies and fifteen gold medals so far."

Kitty went on to win the women's ten-meter diving championships in the 1964 AAU Nationals, and the same year she placed eighth overall in the Olympic Games. "I can do anything," she once told a newspaper reporter. "I like to do things people say I can't do because I'm deaf. I have to work harder than some, but look at the fun I have proving they're wrong."

Kitty began trying other sports, but they were always sports that tested not only her athletic ability but her courage as well. She raced boats and sports cars. She tried skydiving and high-speed waterskiing. In 1970, she set a women's waterskiing speed record, shooting along over a measured course at 104.85 miles per hour.

She competed in off-road automobile and dune-buggy races. She became highly regarded in cross-country motorcycle racing.

Kitty married Duffy Hambleton in 1972. They moved to a large ranch in Fillmore, California. Kitty settled down to being a housewife and mothering Duffy's two teenage children by a previous marriage, a boy and a girl. She worked hard to stay in topflight physical condition, running eight to ten miles every morning. She also lifted weights.

Duffy owned World Wide Enterprises, a firm that rented special-effects equipment to motion picture companies. He also had become a member of Stunts Unlimited, an organization of about thirty stuntmen, and was performing stunts regularly in movies and television.

Kitty became very interested in Duffy's work. She began attending some of his practice sessions and got him to teach her some of the basic stunts—how to fall, fake a fight, and turn a car over. "When she began actually doing all of it, she razzled and dazzled them," Duffy told an interviewer for the *Saturday Evening Post*. "We would only have to explain something once and she'd do it. She's like a computer. She has tremendous powers of concentration."

Kitty began stunting regularly in 1976, appearing on the television series "Bionic Woman." She also appeared on "Quincy" and "Wonder Woman." By 1978, she was receiving more job offers than she could handle and her life story became the subject of a television drama in which she was portrayed by Stockard Channing.

If there is one characteristic that typifies stuntwomen of today and those of earlier times, it is their small number, one piece of evidence that stunting has traditionally been almost as male dominated as, say, professional football. During the 1940s and 1950s, men outnumbered women on about a five-to-one basis, according to Lila Finn, now President of the Stuntwomen of America. The ratio is still about the same.

Stuntwomen were never in demand as much as stuntmen. When a scene called for a female stunt, a stuntman donned a dress and a wig and did it. "It's too dangerous," was the excuse given for not using women to double for women stars.

In recent times, women have been fighting this policy and what Jeannie Epper calls "the automatic attitude many movie people have that such and such a "gag" is too rough for a woman to handle." Roughness has not been a problem for Jeannie herself. She was scooped up in an earthmover and deposited in a dump truck in *Soylent Green,* and depicted being crushed to death by a falling elevator in *Earthquake*.

A group of about twenty women formed the Stunt-

Stuntwoman Victoria Vanderkloot checks an air bag before a leap from Central Park's Belvedere Castle. *(George Sullivan)*

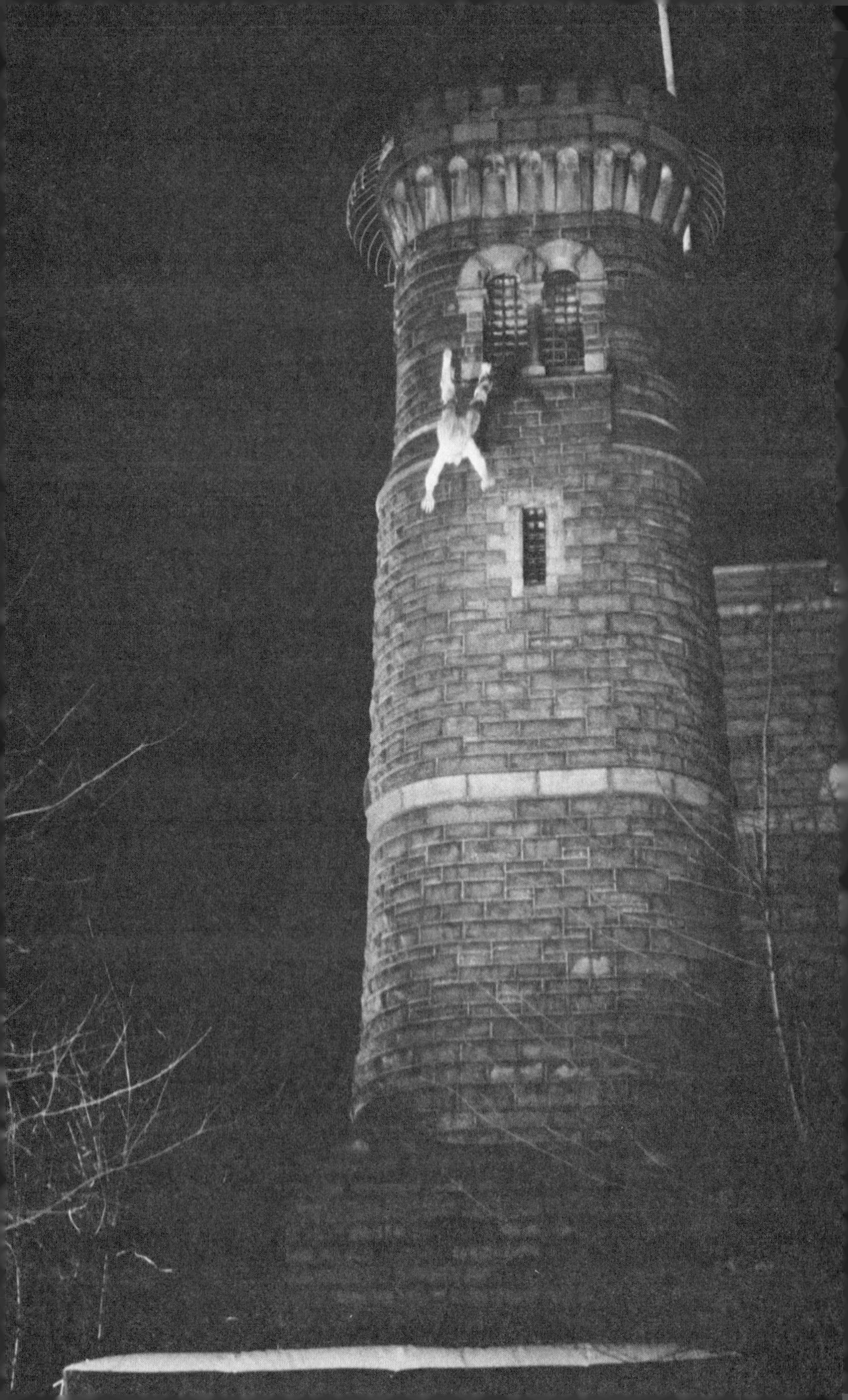

women of America in 1968. In doing so, one of their chief goals was to change industry hiring practices. "I believe that where there is a stunt involving a female character, women should be asked to perform that stunt," said Donna Garrett, one of the organizers of the association.

A "double" was needed to drive a car fast in the film *Mother, Jugs and Speed,* which starred Raquel Welch. Mrs. Garrett, who had doubled for her in other films, asked for the job. She was told she'd be considered. Later she learned that a stuntman had done it. "That's what happens a lot of the time," said Mrs. Garrett. "We hear about a man doubling for a woman after it happens. Women should be asked first. If they don't want to do the stunt, it should be given to a man."

Other women agree. "Women just want to be given the chance to turn the stunt down," says Lila Finn.

Bobby Porter is a twenty-nine-year-old stuntman who often plays movie heroines but stuntwomen never complain. That's because Porter, who stands four-foot-nine, plays kids.

In the movie *Annie,* it was Bobby—not the nine-year-old star of the film, Aileen Quinn—who was pictured dangling from a twenty-story drawbridge waiting to be rescued by Daddy Warbucks. Playing girls is a "rather common occurence" for him, Bobby says.

Bobby Porter notwithstanding, there are a growing number of opportunities for stunt women today. "The guys have been letting the women do more, like turning cars over and such," Julie Johnson, a stuntwoman for fifteen years, told *Ms. Magazine* not long ago. "We're still not doing all we can do. But you can understand their position in a way, because sometimes it's a job where a man has to trust a woman to know she can get that car over in one take; one goof and you've wiped out the whole crew.''

8

Higher, Faster, Hotter

Stuntmen and stuntwomen of the present day are performing feats that never would have been dreamed of in earlier times. They're falling from greater heights and crashing cars at faster speeds. They're enduring real fire for longer periods of time.

They're able to take on tougher assignments because they're relying on modern technology more, calling upon chemical engineers, missile and rocket experts, and specialists in metals and other materials to help them develop the tools of their trade. Some coordinators are even using computers to plan stunts.

But, although the science of stunting has become more sophisticated, it has not become safer. Indeed, the hazards involved may be greater today than ever before.

In the Canadian film *Highpoint,* the director had to find someone who would double for Christopher Plummer in

Dar Robinson holds stunting's free–fall record. (*George Sullivan*)

making a 1,170-foot leap from a ledge at the top of the CN Tower in Toronto, one of the tallest structures in the world. The stunt parachutist who had originally agreed to make the jump had reconsidered, saying that he didn't feel his chances of survival were good enough. The director was thinking of tossing a dummy off the tower when the stunt coordinator, Carey Loftin, put in a call to Dar Robinson, a thirty-two-year-old stuntman from Los Angeles, the holder of nine stunting records. The idea of doing the jump appealed to Dar. The money involved may also have helped to convince him. Dar won't reveal the exact amount he received, but it is believed to be about 150 thousand dollars.

Once he had agreed to do the stunt, Dar's first step was to meet with Jim Handbury of Advanced Air Sports Products in Lake Elsinore, California, a company that specializes in designing parachutes for skydivers and hang-gliding enthusiasts. "We've learned a great deal about parachutes in the last five years," says Handbury. "Skydivers, not engineers, are designing parachutes. They open quickly, help provide for accurate landings, and give fast horizontal movement across the sky."

The parachute with which Dar was provided had a pilot chute so small that Dar was able to carry it in a side pocket of his trousers. To deploy the main chute, Dar simply reached into his pocket, pulled out the pilot chute, and unfurled it. "It was like reaching for a hankie," Dar says.

Dar mapped out his jump strategy carefully, planning how many feet he would be in free-fall, how many feet he would fall while deploying his chute, and how many feet he would fall while deployment was taking place. He was able to determine almost the exact point at which the chute would open.

Dar tested the chute from low-flying airplanes, making his leap, counting to five, then deploying the chute and riding it down. On one test jump, he couldn't get the chute to open (a packing loop was still tied around it), and he had to rely on his reserve chute. The very next day he suffered another chute malfunction, and again the reserve chute saved him. Then, just three weeks before the Tower jump, a close friend of Dar's was killed in a sky-diving accident. Dar was not in a confident frame of mind as the day of the jump drew near. "I'll tell you," he said, "the day before I was to make the jump, I walked through the streets of Toronto wondering if this was the last day I was going to live."

When the day of the jump arrived, Dar had some misgivings. At the top of the tower, he looked out, then checked his equipment, and checked it again. He checked it four times, in fact. He briefly considered packing up his gear and leaving, not doing the stunt at all. But he realized that he was obligated to do it, and if he abandoned the project now, it would ruin his career. "No one would ever be willing to hire me again," he said.

The cameras were poised. The director said, "Action." Dar hopped up onto the ledge and without a second's hesitation stepped off.

"They wanted five seconds of free-fall," Dar recalls. "I gave them one more second than they wanted. I gave them six seconds."

People on the ground who were watching screamed at

the top of their lungs. Carey Loftin called it "a horrible nightmare."

"After the six seconds of free-fall, there was one second of reaction time," Dar recalls, "and then two more seconds in getting the chute to deploy. At that point, I was at a level of three hundred to three hundred and fifty feet, a little more than one second off the ground. That's just the way I planned it."

Dar's feat caused headlines from coast to coast. It wasn't the first time he had won national acclaim. Dar once drove an MG automobile out of a cargo plane at 13,500 feet, put the car into a free fall, deployed a parachute that floated the car to the ground, and then drove away.

"I do the tough stuff, not the "gravy jobs," Dar says. "They never call me to do a foot fall, fall down the stairs, or a fight scene—the easy stuff. People are beginning to say I'm another Evel Knievel."

Another time, Dar jumped out of a plane, went into a free-fall for over a mile, and alighted on another airplane, and he did it without using a parachute. How was it possible to do such a stunt? The second plane was in a nose-down dive at the time, its speed controlled by a drogue chute at 125 miles per hour. Dar caught up to the falling aircraft, got onto a wing, climbed into the cockpit, released the chute, and flew off.

"Is there any stunt that you wouldn't do?" Dar is often asked in interviews. He has a standard answer. "Sure there is," he says with a grin, "I just haven't run across it yet."

High falls of more modest distances than those recently

attempted by Dar Robinson have also been affected by modern technology. Stunt people used to do falls of up to sixty or seventy feet into cardboard boxes. Several layers of boxes would be piled up high and, then thick mattresses would be placed on top of the stack. The stuntman would leap into the mattresses. The stuntman Tony Leonard once dived seventy-eight feet into piled-up boxes.

Another method was to lay several long boards, each twelve inches wide and one inch thick, across a pair of sawhorses. Mattresses would be placed on top of and under the boards. When the stuntman plunged into the mattresses, the boards would bend almost to the point of snapping, absorbing the impact of the jump.

All such methods have given way to the air landing pad, or air bag, which came into widespread use during the mid-1970s. A typical nylon-covered air bag is fifteen feet wide, twenty feet long, and three to six feet high, approximately the size of a small swimming pool.

The bag is inflated with warm air from an electrically powered fan. At impact, sealed vents in the sides of the bag burst open, letting the air slowly escape. This cushions the stuntman's leap.

The air bag was developed by the stuntman Bob Yerkes, who began working on it in 1965. Dar Robinson helped Yerkes test the pad by safely leaping into it from heights exceeding one hundred feet. Air bags are used not only for stunt work. Fire departments in every part of the country

On impact, air bag vents like this one burst open, allowing air to escape and cushioning the fall. *(George Sullivan)*

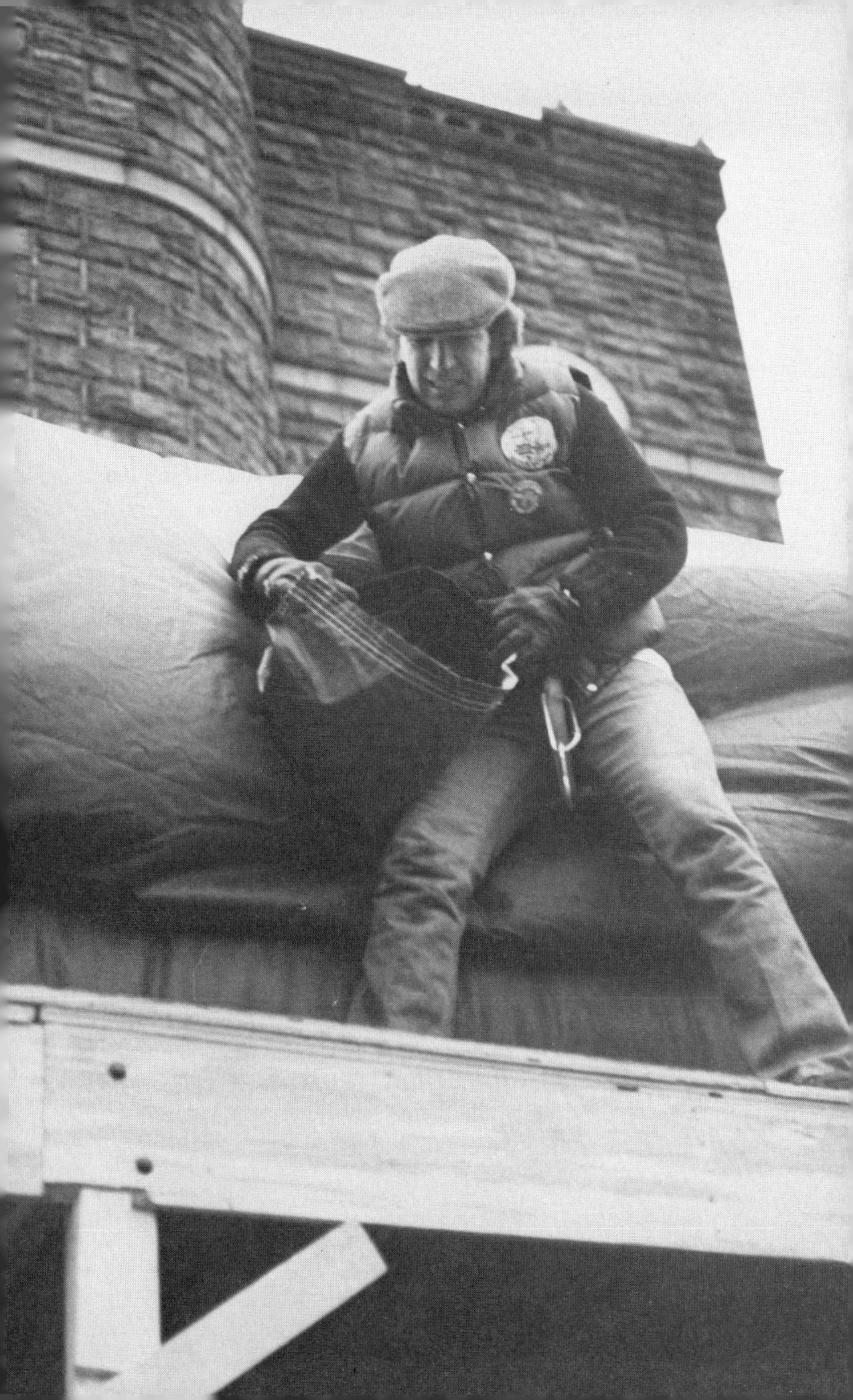

are acquiring them for rescuing victims from the upper floors of burning buildings.

Up until fairly recent times, the method of turning over a car was to drive the wheels on one side up a ramp that was hidden from the camera. As soon as that side of the car was elevated high enough, the vehicle flipped over.

Today, a "cannon" is used. The cannon is a large cylinder which is welded underneath the car. Into it fits a heavy projectile the size of a sawed-off telephone pole. The muzzle of the cannon points down toward the pavement. Blasting powder goes inside the cylinder.

The stuntman drives the car along the roadway. When he comes to the spot where he wants the car to turn over, he throws it into a sideways skid and hits a button on the dashboard. The cylinder fires like a cannon, driving the projectile into the pavement and flipping the car over.

Stunts involving horses are usually much different today than they used to be. The Running W, a device used to make a horse fall, is no longer in use, (or at least it's not supposed to be). The American Humane Association has been successful in having the Running W outlawed.

Instead, horses are trained to fall on cue. But training a horse to fall isn't as humane as is generally believed. The trainer begins by tying one of the horse's front legs to a rope on a pulley. When the horse is standing still, the trainer pulls the horse's leg up, draws his head to one side, and gets the animal to lie down gently. The drill is repeated over and over, with the trainer attempting to show the horse that doing the exercise doesn't hurt in the slightest.

Once the horse is able to do the stunt from a standing-still position, the trainer walks the horse slowly, pulls the

Higher, Faster, Hotter

leg with the rope, draws the horse's head around, and lays the animal down. This is repeated over and over. The horse eventually realizes that when the trainer draws his head around, he wants him to fall. The next step, of course, is to get the horse to gallop and fall.

While falling on cue sounds kinder for the horse than the Running W, some trainers say it's not. "The only reason the horse falls is because it knows it's going to get hurt in the mouth if it doesn't," says one trainer. "The horse is being abused, but few people realize this."

Sometimes it's more convenient or less expensive to use a Running W. "We have to be on the watch all the time," says a spokesperson for the American Humane Association. "A director will pull out a Running W when there's no one from our organization around. We suspect that Running W's were used three times in the last couple of months of 1979."

In most cases, there is close cooperation between the American Humane Association and the major film-producing studios and three television networks. Scripts for productions involving animal action are sent to the Hollywood office of the AHA for review to determine whether safety standards have been met.

Once filming begins, a field representative of the AHA assists and advises the producer and director. It is his or her responsibility to insist that terrain for a horse run or stampede is free of rocks, stumps, fallen trees, ditches, and potholes. If a horse is to run down an embankment, the AHA representative makes sure that it is not so steep that a fall might occur.

When a horse rears up, the AHA wants a front-feet

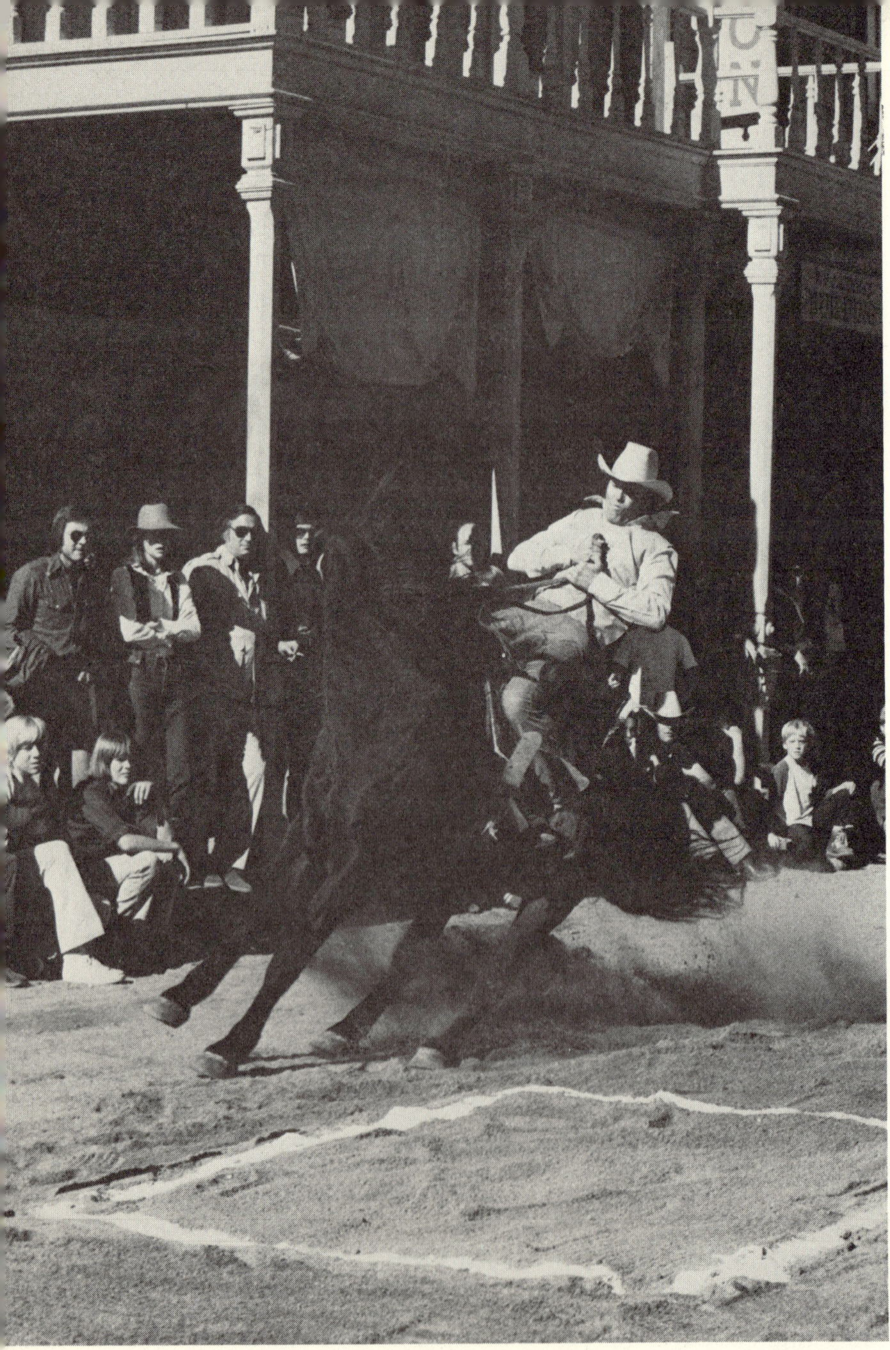

Here is the proper way to execute a horse fall—without injury to the rider or horse. *(CBS-TV)*

landing, and no going over backwards. When a horse runs on pavement, the AHA sees to it that the animal wears special shoes for sure footing. When a horse is called upon to leap over a hurdle, the topmost part of the structure must be of breakaway construction.

Runaway wagons and stage coaches that tip over must be rigged to allow the team to run free. If the driver is to be "shot" and to fall off the rig, the AHA demands the presence of a second driver (who is usually concealed beneath the seat) to guide the horses to a safe stop.

The AHA representative keeps an eye on the feeding, watering, and corralling of the horses. There are similar AHA guidelines to protect other animals.

There are still problems, however. In 1966, filmmakers dropped sections of the Motion Picture Production Code that referred to animals. Along about the same time, production companies began leaving Hollywood to film at locations outside the United States. Today they are scattered all over the globe.

Thus, it is not always possible for an AHA representative to be present during filming. In addition, since the supervision is no longer made mandatory by the Motion Picture Production Code, the AHA does not always receive the scripts in advance.

The result has been an increase in animal abuse. "They Kill Animals and They Call It Art" was the title of an article in *The New York Times* that cited the increased number of films that stress "realism" at the expense of animal life. Said the article: "More and more directors are using the deaths of innocent creatures to provide shocks their films might otherwise fail to deliver."

The American Humane Association has established a rating system that is meant to alert the movie-going public to films containing objectionable animal treatment. Films are classified as "acceptable" or "unacceptable," depending on the treatment given animals.

In 1982, the AHA called for the public to boycott the film *Conan, the Barbarian* because of its "needless cruelty to the performing animals." Said the AHA: "There are horrendous horse trips, a dog is kicked by a warrior, and a camel stricken down."

The AHA agrees that boycotts and their system of film ratings is not going to solve the problem. Animal abuse remains an alarming trend in the movie industry.

Modern day fire stunts, such as those featured in *The Hindenberg* and *The Towering Inferno,* are performed very realistically, thanks to a wide variety of new equipment. In *The Hindenberg,* for example, where nine stuntpeople were "burned alive," each performer wore nomex underwear, an outer garment made of a tough, fibrous material that was half an inch thick, an asbestos face mask, and over that, a rubber mask of the human face. Each stunt person also carried a hidden oxygen supply, similar to the scuba system an underwater diver wears. It contained enough oxygen for three minutes of trouble-free breathing.

When the cameras were rolling, the stunt people's clothing was saturated with alcohol and then ignited. No scene could be more than three minutes in length, because no one could stay within the burning suit any longer than that. Otherwise, he or she would have been baked to death.

The trouble with special suits, masks, and oxygen equipment is that they give the wearer a bulky look. This problem can be solved to some extent by using a special gel, the development of forty-year-old Grant Page, an Australian who has been a stuntman for more than twenty years. When doing a fire stunt, Grant dons a woolen jump suit that has been soaked in the gel. He covers his face and hair with it, smearing it on like cold cream. The gel is colorless, but on camera it looks like sweat.

Over the jump suit, Page puts on regular clothing, whatever costume the film requires him to wear. The

This fire stunt was featured in *The Hindenburg*. (*Movie Star News*)

clothing is then covered with airplane glue, rubber cement, or some other highly flammable substance. Other stuntmen, holding wet blankets, stand nearby. After being ignited, Page's clothing burns long enough for the cameras to record the scene, and then the other stuntmen leap forward and smother the flames with their blankets.

"Timing is important," says Page. "The flames will go on for as long as the clothes last. Actually, you can ruin a shot by letting the burning go on too long. You end up without any clothes left.

"The gel isn't magic. It doesn't stop burning. It increases the body's tolerance to heat, so that you can burn four or five times as long."

Page, who says it took him eight years to learn to work with the gel, has done almost one hundred fire stunts. In 1979, he was the stunt coordinator in the making of *City on Fire*, which boasted a cast that included Henry Fonda and Shelley Winters. In one scene, Page directed 150 extras who were engulfed in flames. "Not one person got so much as a singed eyebrow," Page says. He himself did stunts as six different fire victims in the film.

The gel is not the product of some space-age laboratory; quite the opposite. It is made from the sap of the ti, a tropical palmlike plant. According to Page, aborigines in Australia have been using the gel for more than a thousand years. When an aborigine burns himself, he slashes open a ti plant and holds the burned part next to the sap, getting instant relief from pain and shock.

The gel is now widely used in Australia for treating burn victims. "It's remarkable what it can do," says Page. "It creates a vapor shield between the flames and the user's body. It reduces shock. It lowers body temperature. It stops tissue from burning."

Page has performed stunts in more than forty movies since 1975, and not just fire stunts. He's jumped off cliffs, been knocked down by cars, and crashed through windows. But as a concession to his age, Page has stopped doing car knockdowns, and he's lowered the limit on how high he'll fall. "The bruises are too much for a man my age," he says. Fire stunts are different. "I don't see why

I'll ever have to stop doing them," he says. "I can do fire stunts until the day I die."

When a film audience sees an actor being exploded into the air, there's really no explosion at all, just the sound of an explosion and perhaps a brief, sudden burst of light created by flash powder. The stunt person doubling for the actor is actually jerked into the air by means of a telescoping ratchet that is powered by a nitrogen-driven piston. The ratchet is connected by thin but very strong wire to a shoulder harness the stunt person wears. Originally developed for use in connection with airplane landing systems, the equipment can be rigged so that the stunt person is "exploded" horizontally as well as vertically.

Of course, to work with the equipment, a stuntman has to be skilled and experienced in how to land, and he must wear proper protective padding—a jockstrap and cup, hip and thigh pads, rib pads, a padded corset, shoulder pads, and a skullcap inside his hat or wig. He also wears a heavy pad on what is known as his "quitting arm," the arm which he throws out to break his fall. All such pads are now made of foam rubber, an enormous improvement over kapok pads of the past.

Strong wire and cables have been important to stunting since the days of the Keystone Kops. Thanks to advances pioneered in the aircraft industry, cables now offer greater tensile strength than ever before. A new rubber compound has led to the development of "shock cord," a cable that permits a stunt person to bob up and down like a human yo-yo within a range of thirty feet.

Technical advances in the field of chemistry have al-

Cables of super strength are used in creating stunts such as this one.
(Harry Madsen)

tered the "glass" through which stunt people crash. For decades, the substitute for real glass was a kind of candy, a transparent sugar-based mixture that was rolled out to windowpane thickness and allowed to harden. These candy windows melted under hot studio lights. The sheet glass moviemakers use today is a special plastic. When it shatters, it looks like glass, but it has none of the hazards of the real thing.

When the General Motors Corporation asked Hal Needham to jump a pickup truck over a lake and land it safely on the other side, for a scene to be used in an industrial film the company was making, Needham consulted missile

Higher, Faster, Hotter

experts. They suggested a rocket engine for the truck, one that generated fifteen thousand horsepower in five-thousandths of a second.

Needham did the stunt successfully, later saying it wasn't particularly difficult. "It was the kind of stunt," he said, "in which you can work everything out in advance. You know how far you have to go. You know how high. Then you simply figure out how much power you must

Glass used by moviemakers has none of the hazards of the real thing. This is stuntman Harry Madsen. *(Harry Madsen)*

develop to cover that distance. Then it's just a matter of doing it."

New technical developments, however, have not made stunting any less hazardous. Indeed, many observers believe that quite the opposite is true.

"Nobody before would've considered being able to roll a car more than a couple of times," Ron Rendell, a stunt coordinator on a number of movies and television shows, once said. "Now, with cannons, you can turn these cars over indefinitely on flat ground. I feel that, if anything, the business has gotten *more* dangerous in the last ten years."

Another element is also serving to increase the risks. It is the struggle among filmmakers and television producers to outdo one another in terms of thrills and excitement. As James Nissen, an official of the Screen Actors Guild, told *The New York Times* in 1982: "When a director jumps a car fifty feet in one picture, the director of the next movie says, 'Let's do it higher and longer.' When one director has a fifteen-foot-high explosion, the next director wants a twenty-five-foot-high explosion."

Many observers believe that this attitude was a contributing factor in a series of accidents that injured or killed nearly a dozen stunt people, camera operators, and actors during the late 1970s and early 1980s.

Stuntman Jim Shepherd was killed by being dragged behind a horse during the filming of *Comes a Horseman* in 1977. Stuntman A. J. Bakunas did a 323-foot fall for the film *Steel*. His air bag malfunctioned and collapsed and Bakunas was killed. A car swerved the wrong way during production on *Cannonball Run* in June 1980, and twenty-five-year-old Heidi Von Beltz, a stunt woman for only a short time, was paralyzed.

In the spring of 1981, Jack Tanberg was hit and killed by a runaway car on the set of *The Five of Me*. The same year, in *The Sword and the Sorcerer,* stuntman Jack Tyree missed the airbag onto which he was to have jumped and was killed. On the TV series *Code Red,* also in 1981, stuntman Victor Hunsberger partially missed his air bag, slammed his head onto concrete, and was severely injured.

The increasing use of helicopters has led to several tragic accidents. A director, Boris Sagal, was killed during the production of his television movie, *World War II,* when he walked into a helicopter blade in May 1981.

The worst accident in years took place in July 1982 when Vic Morrow and two children were killed in a helicopter crash. It took place on the set of the *Twilight Zone* Movie.

After that accident, stunt people, actors, and crew members began to protest what they felt were unsafe working conditions. Some placed the blame for the rash of accidents on film directors. It is the director who makes the final decision on whether a planned stunt is safe. It has been suggested that decision should rest with the stunt coordinator.

There is no easy solution. Safety guidelines are being carefully studied by the Screen Actors Guild, Screen Extras Guild, Directors Guild, and camera and sound unions, and their recommendations are awaited.

9

So You Want to Be a Stunt Person

Someone once asked Dar Robinson what advice he had for the boy or girl whose ambition it was to be a stunt person. "I'll tell you," said Dar, "if you're thinking of becoming a stuntman or woman, the best advice I can give you is to forget it."

Most other stunt people have the same advice, and it's not because they consider what they do to be especially dangerous. Indeed, they say the easiest part of their professional lives is being slammed into walls or knocked down stairs, and taking high dives off tall buildings. Finding work is what's difficult, even if you're highly qualified and experienced. The field of stunting is terribly overcrowded, with many more people available than jobs.

The situation doesn't prevent thousands of young people from attempting to make the grade each year. All but a small handful end up disappointed. "It's like a high school football player dreaming about becoming quarterback for the Pittsburgh Steelers," one stuntman points out. "There's only one job like that in the whole universe. A lot of young people aren't realistic about what it's practical for them to achieve. They end up with shattered dreams."

" 'Don't quit school.' That's the first thing I tell boys or girls who come to me wanting to be stunt people," says Alex Stevens, a noted East coast stuntman. "Study, I tell them. Take plenty of courses in physics. Learn about velocities, impact forces, aerodynamics, thermodynamics, and hydrodynamics. All of these apply to stunting.

"I tell them to learn about cameras and lenses. Even still photography can teach you a lot.

"Go out for sports. Get involved with the gymnastics team, if your school has one. Do some trampoline work and tumbling. Some track and field events are good, too. Pole-vaulting, for instance. And all the running you'll be doing keeps you in shape.

"Join the dramatics club or take acting courses, if they're available. Stunt people when they're doubling have to be actors, you know. And it's not at all unusual for a stuntman or woman to have a speaking role."

Some youngsters who aspire to be stunt people feel their fearlessness is what qualifies them. They're not afraid to jump off a roof into an old mattress. They're not afraid to put an automobile into a spin.

Actually, there's nothing wrong with a little fear. "I feel those butterflies start fluttering everytime I do an important 'gag,' " one stuntman says. "But that's good. Fear makes me careful. It gives me respect for what can happen. Fear is what keeps me alive."

Everyone agrees that having athletic ability is vital for becoming a stunt person. Dar Robinson, for example, was trained in gymnastics—specifically in trampoline work—as a young boy. He competed nationally in trampolining and holds the trampoline jumping record—forty feet. Dar was also a circus performer. He had a tumbling act and a clown act, and he did some trapeze and high-wire work—"a little bit of everything," he says. Dar also raced motorcycles professionally.

"Training in gymnastics is the best," says Harry Madsen of New York, a stuntman for ten years. "It assures the flexibility that stunting demands. And experience in gymnastics gives you an awareness of what your body is doing, where the various parts are positioned when you're doing a flip or a high fall."

Some individuals were rodeo performers before turning to stunting. Others have had experience as race car drivers. Hal Needham was a treetopper and tested parachutes before he became a stuntman.

Grant Page, who has worked in more than fifty films and performed hundreds of stunts, majored in physical education in college and then joined the commandos, a specially trained military unit used for surprise attacks and destructive raids. As a commando, Page was trained in parachute jumping and cliff work, and he served as a diving instructor. He also studied physics. By the time he was ready to take up a career in stunting, he had half a lifetime of training.

Physical training is only part of it. "I think that having the ability to concentrate is more important than anything else," says Harry Madsen. "When you're about to do a 'gag,' you have to be able to wipe everything else out of your mind, and focus your thinking on what you have to do.

"You also have to have the ability to take instruction. When the director or stunt coordinator says, 'Here's what I want you to do,' well, you have to be able to do exactly that, with no variations."

Although it's often overlooked by those with ambitions to be stunt people, it's also important to know how physical forces interact. You have to know how to design, construct, and operate mechanical structures. "Someone came to me not long ago," Dar Robinson recalls, "and said that he wanted me to jump a motorcycle off a ramp, catapulting it high into the air, and then I was supposed to parachute from the motorcycle to the ground. The person that designed the stunt had recommended a ramp with a thirty-eight degree incline. That's much too steep of an angle. The G forces would have been too great. Most of the jobs that I have of that kind involve a ramp angle of about eleven degrees. There were other things about the stunt that I didn't like. You have to know these things. Your life depends on it."

There are no books about stunting that an apprentice can study. One learns through experience. "And you never stop learning," says Alex Stevens. "Every stunt you do teaches you something because every stunt is different. Take stair falls, for instance. A stair fall in a house is not the same as a stair fall in the subway. The size of the stairs and the height of the risers make a difference. What the stairs are made of is important. The width and steepness of

So You Want to Be a Stunt Person

the stairway are factors, too. Everytime you do a stair fall, you add to your knowledge."

In 1979, a stunt school was established in Chatsworth, California by the stuntman Kim Kahana to train individuals in stair falls, high falls, horsebackriding, fisticuffs, car hits, the use of weapons, and the other specialties common to stunting. In his early fifties, Kahana had been involved in stunt work for more than twenty-five years and had appeared in hundreds of motion pictures and television shows. Kahana had become a stuntman by accident. He went with a friend who was being interviewed for a job performing a motorcycle stunt in the film *The Wild Ones*. Kahana, who was skilled in driving motorcycles, too, also happened to be interviewed—and landed the job. He has

Classroom instruction at Kahana's Stunt School is serious business. (*Kahana's Stunt School*)

worked with such stars as Clint Eastwood, James Caan, James Garner, and Robert Wagner. A native of Hawaii, Kahana is also an expert in the martial arts, holding black belts in karate, jujitsu, and aikido, a Japanese form of self-defense.

The school has been approved by the California Board of Education. For a fee of fifteen hundred dollars, each student attends six daylong classes on consecutive Saturdays at Kahana's ranch, which is equipped with high towers, air bags, trampolines, and mats. Trained horses and specially equipped automobiles are also available.

Classes are kept small, with no more than ten or twelve students in each. About one-half of the students are women. Students are graded in each course. Get a "D" in High Falls and you're probably a candidate for a broken leg.

Kahana rejects well over half of the applications he receives. "A prospective student must really be serious about studying stunt work," he says. "I restrict the school to people who want to make stunts their full-time profession. That's the only type of person I'm interested in accepting."

Athletic ability is also important. "You've got to be in topnotch physical condition," Kahana says. "But more than physical ability, I look for the right attitude. You can't be an egomaniac, concerned only with your own glory. This can be a life-and-death business. There are times a stuntman is responsible for another person's life, as well as his own. It's no game."

Each training session begins with an hour-long period of stretching exercises and then a mile run. First, each student learns to fall down. "Ninety percent of all stunt work is falls and fights," says Kahana. "They're boring, but you've got to get your timing on the mat before you can try going off a motorcycle or a horse or onto a studio's cement floor."

Instead of executing a forward somersault when falling, which can lead to a head or neck injury, students are taught to touch down gently with their hands, turn the head to one side, and roll onto one shoulder.

Little by little, Kahana keeps making the falls more difficult. He places a round bag in front of the mat, then instructs each student to dive over the bag and into a shoulder roll. Then he removes the bag and places two chairs side by side in front of the mat, and signals each student to run and jump over them. Next, students learn to take a running start, jump onto a trampoline, and go into a shoulder roll while in midair. They also learn how to fall backward.

The class the following week is devoted to studio fights, barroom brawls, and karate competition. The basic film punches, Kahana explains, are the roundhouse right and short blow to the gut. To throw a roundhouse right, you step with the right foot, and without bending the elbow, swing the right arm and fist toward your target in the widest possible arc. "Get your body into it," Kahana tells a student.

Of course, the punch never really connects, missing the opponent's chin by an inch or so. The opponent reacts by taking two or three stumbling steps backward or by executing a back fall.

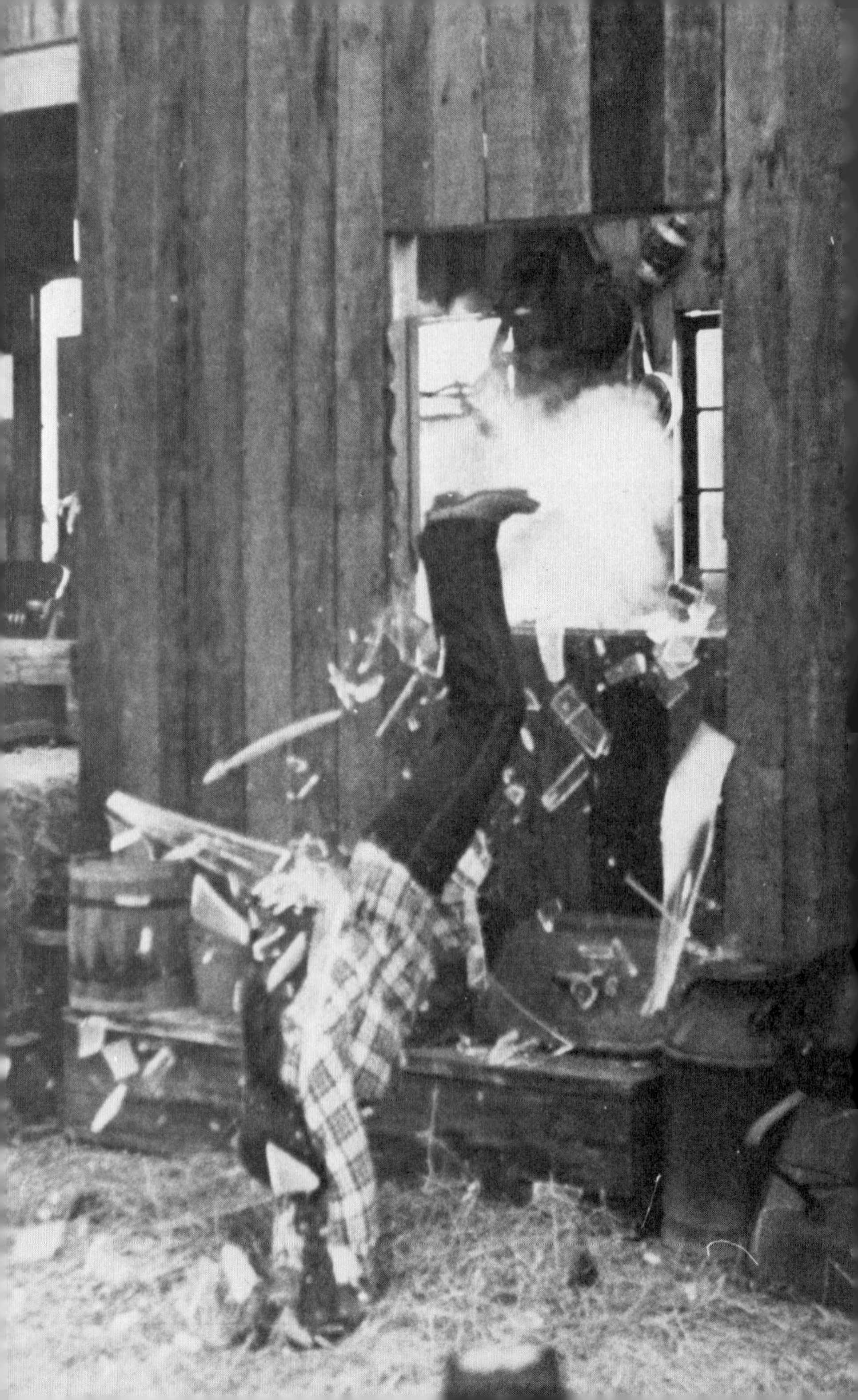

Next, the students learn to do high falls, leaping down twenty-five feet from the roof of a building onto a big air bag. While the bag is capable of safely cushioning a two-hundred foot jump, each student has to land right. Even a twenty-five-foot fall can cause a broken back or leg, should the student fail to hit the cushion properly.

The first leap each student takes is called a "Suicide." For this you must lean back and extend your legs straight out so that you land flat on your rear. "What you mustn't do is hit the bag feet first," one of the instructors cautions a student. "You can break your legs with that kind of landing, or your knees can come up and smash into your face."

Week No. 4 of the course is devoted to horseback, to learning various stunt mounts. The crouper is the most common. (The "croup" is the highest point of the horse's rump.) From a running start about twenty feet behind the horse, you dash forward, placing both hands on the horse's rear, and then vault upward and into the saddle.

The crouper can be risky unless the horse knows you're coming. "Before you start," an instructor advises, "be sure the horse's feet are together so he can't kick you."

The day for the instruction titled Car Hits involves the use of Kahana's old white Chevrolet Impala. Mats are placed along each side of the car, and the driver eases it ahead at a speed of about five miles per hour. Each student, in turn, gets sideswiped by the oncoming automobile and flipped over the hood. "The key to this stunt is the

Fights and falls are included in the curriculum. (*Kahana's Stunt School*)

basic shoulder-roll technique," says Kahana. "When the car makes contact, you leap onto the hood and shoulder-roll your way across, going off on the other side onto the mat.

"Remember to keep your feet up, and the forward motion of the car will carry you through."

Weapons and firearms are covered in the final week of instruction. "If you're doing a war picture or a Western, you've got to know how to shoot a gun," says Kahana. The morning of the last day is given over to the firing of various types of weapons, with students using live ammunition.

In the afternoon, a bomb explosion is staged. Students are the "victims." A minitrampoline is concealed in some bushes. On a prearranged signal, two students take a running start and leap onto the trampoline. The instant they hit, a timing device ignites some flash powder. Smoke billows up. Big rocks—chunks of cork, actually—go flying thrugh the air. So do the students, each landing with a smooth shoulder roll.

Kahana's twenty-year-old daughter Debbie is one of the school's more successful graduates. She had been seen falling, fighting, and catching afire in such feature films as *Earthquake, Two Minute Warning* and *Chesty Anderson, U.S. Navy.* She has also performed stunts in such television series as "Marcus Welby, M.D.," "Little House on the Prairie," and "Kids Are People, Too."

To keep in shape, Debbie lifts weights, jogs, and prac-

Students must also become skilled in karate.

(*Kahana's Stunt School*)

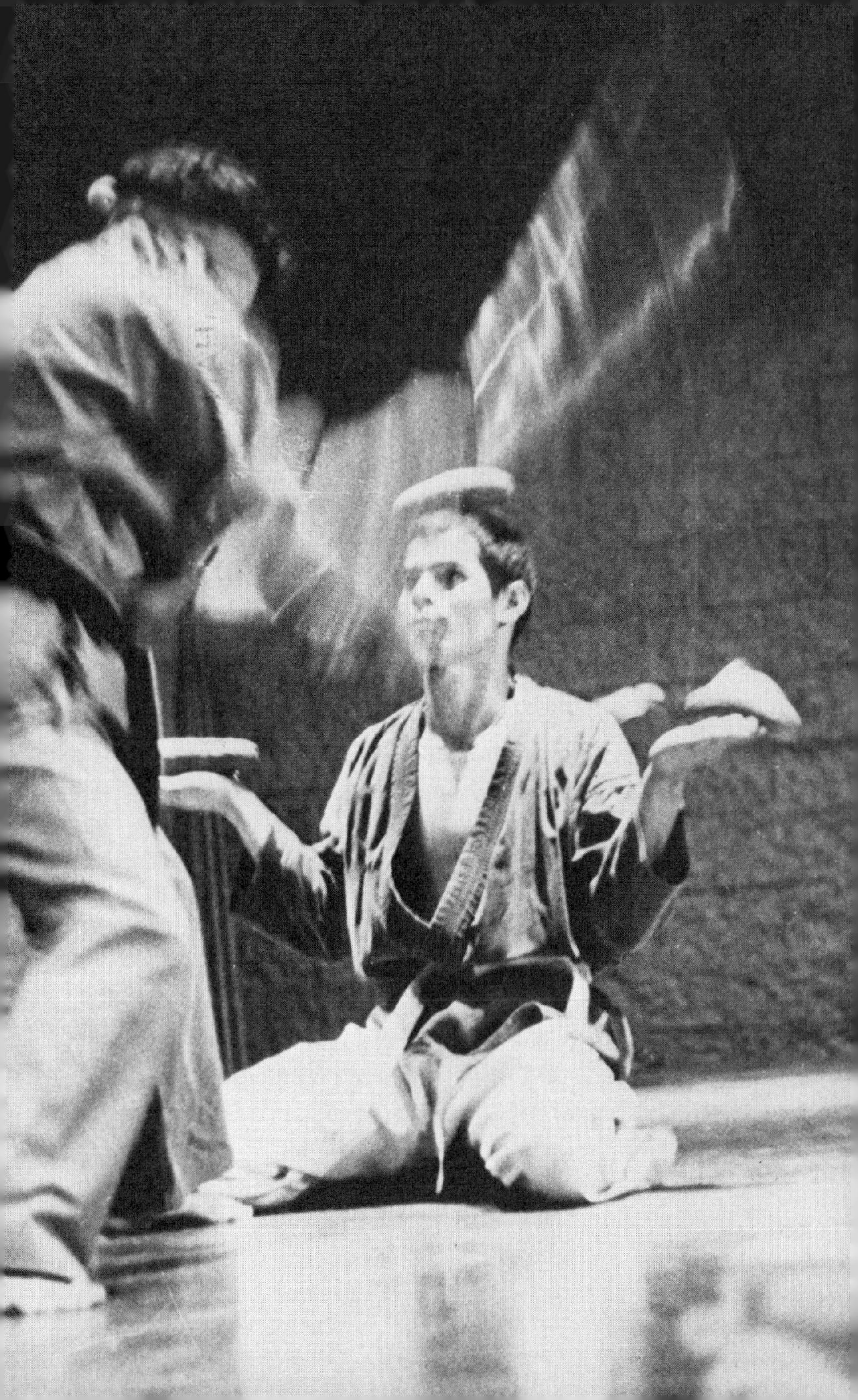

tices karate. Mr. Kahana began teaching Debbie karate when she was ten. She now holds a third-degree black belt.

Debbie's only serious accident occurred while practicing a horseback-riding stunt. It called for her to take a fall into a soft dirt pile. But, as Debbie put the horse into a gallop, the rope ran out and jerked her out of the saddle too soon. Instead of falling into soft dirt, she landed painfully on hard ground. No bones were broken but her back was badly bruised.

Debbie's small size—she stands four-foot-eleven and weighs 90 pounds—often helps her to earn work doubling for children. (Stunt kids are a great rarity.) "The trick to staying active in the stunt business," Debbie once said, "is to find an actress you resemble and become her regular stand-in." But doubling for kids doesn't present any such opportunity. "They all keep outgrowing me," Debbie says.

Debbie's father is quick to point out that completion of his training course in no way guarantees employment in motion pictures or television. "In fact," he declares, "I try to discourage people from getting into the business, because we have, in my opinion, too many people already.

"You have to be aggressive, very aggressive, to make it as a stuntman or woman, aggressive, that is, when it comes to looking for work. You can't be inhibited. You've got to get out and talk to people. Sure, people are going to say you're pushy. But if you don't push, you won't make it."

Those men and women who do eventually "make it" as stunt people earn a weekly base pay of 1,114 dollars, an amount established by the Screen Actors Guild. All stunt people belong to SAG, as it's called.

In addition to their base pay, stunt people receive additional fees for each stunt they perform. These fees, which are negotiated beforehand, range from twenty-five to one thousand dollars and more. Perhaps as many as a dozen stunt people earn upwards of one hundred thousand dollars annually.

Many of the more knowledgeable and experienced stunt people become stunt coordinators. A stunt coordinator is the individual responsible for stunts during the production of a motion picture or television show. After reading the script and conferring with other people involved in the production, the coordinator designs the action and hires the stuntmen and stuntwomen. Sometimes the coordinator performs some of the more difficult stunts.

"A stunt coordinator is like an extension of the director's arm," says Dar Robinson. "The director says, 'This is what I need,' and then it's up to me as the stunt coordinator to fill that need. I know the capabilities of the various stunt people. I pick the right man or woman for the job.

"In the weeks before the filming begins, I work with the other departments, with the wardrobe department, getting the right clothing for the stunt people, and with the makeup department. I help scout the locations we'll be using."

Robinson was the stunt coordinator on *Hawks,* a film produced in 1980 that starred Sylvester Stallone. One of the film's fight scenes involved three stuntmen and the two principals, Stallone and Billy Dee Williams.

"The script simply tells us what happens, who's fighting and the outcome," Robinson said. "We have to put it all together, lay it out in sequence. It's like putting steps to music, only it's more difficult. You have to be concerned with facial expressions, with movement, with having the scene flow well. And it all has to look authentic.

"You have to know what the camera sees. Some punches will 'sell' to the camera; others are a 'miss.'

"If I were to fight someone in a real fight, and I used the tactics I use in a motion picture fight, the guy would kill me. You have to draw your fist way back to throw a punch for the camera; you have to telegraph your punches. Everything is slowed down. The camera doesn't pick up fast punches."

Perspective is important, too. We see everything in three dimensions. A camera doesn't. It sees things in two dimensions.

A director can use this to his advantage. "Suppose I'm six-foot-two," says Dar Robinson, "and for a film that's being shot, I'm to fight a man who's five-foot-six. The director wants the shorter man to appear about the same height I am, so it doesn't look like I'm going to beat the stuffing out of him. All he has to do is keep the shorter man close to the camera—"up camera"—as we punch away, and position me back, away from the camera. We'll appear to be the same height in the film."

Stuntmen and stuntwomen have formed several organizations for their mutual benefit. The largest is the Stuntmen's Association of Motion Pictures. The organization, which dates to 1961, was founded by stuntmen Dick Geary and Loren Jones. About fifty stuntmen joined immediately. The organization has about 125 members today.

In order to qualify for membership, an individual must

So You Want to Be a Stunt Person

be a member of the Screen Actors Guild for at least three years. (In order to become a member of the Guild, you must have received employment from a motion picture or television production company that is recognized by the Guild.)

"There are no schools to teach one how to become a stuntman," according to Rock Walker, president of the Stuntmen's Association. "However, an extensive athletic background would be helpful, and a liking for self-motivated hustle is mandatory."

Hal Needham and two of his associates formed Stunts Unlimited in 1970. About forty stuntmen belong to Need-

Hal Needham and two associates founded Stunts Unlimited in 1970.
(*Movie Star News*)

ham's organization. Besides providing stuntmen for motion pictures and television, Stunts Unlimited rents equipment to production companies and supervises stunt sequences. It is the only organization to provide these services.

For stunt women, there are two organizations, the Stuntwomen of America and the Society of Professional Stuntwomen. Their total membership is less than thirty.

The Black Stuntmen's Association, composed of women as well as men, was formed in 1968 by a dozen former athletes, all Californians. For many years, whites traditionally performed stunts—using blackfaces—that logically should have gone to blacks. "Now blacks want to do stunts for whites, increasing the opportunity for work," says Ernie Robinson, director of a training program sponsored by the Black Stuntmen's Association. "It's not as unreasonable as it sounds. Makeup men can accomplish just about anything."

In the eastern United States, there is the East Coast Stuntmen's Association and the Professional Stuntmen's Federation. Both organizations are based in New York City.

One stuntman estimates that five thousand young men and women try to become professional stunters every year. Of these five thousand, only a small handful are successful. But those men and women who eventually enter that select circle of one hundred who do most of the stunting for motion pictures and television universally agree the struggle is worthwhile. "I'll never quit, no matter how much money I have," says one veteran stuntman. "My body demands stunting. I think maybe my ego does, too."

Index

Adversaries, The, 92
Air Mail, 85
"Airport '77," 11
American Magazine, The, 44
American Youth Magazine, 130
Anderson, Broncho Billy, 46
Anderson, Judith, 118, 127
Annie, 135
Arbuckle, Roscoe (Fatty), 28, 32
Autry, Gene, 51, 61-2

B-17 bomber stunts, 87-8
B-25 bomber stunts, 92
"B.A.D.Cats," 115
Bangville Police, The, 21
Bank Dick, The, 106
"Baretta," 9
"Barnstormers," 68
Barthelmess, Richard, 30, 83
Beechcraft stunts, 90-1
Ben Hur, 63
Biograph Company, 18-19, 30
"Bionic Woman," 11, 132
Birth of a Nation, 67
Black Cats, The, 77
"Black Sheep Squadron," 92
Black Stuntmen's Association, 172-73
Blondell, Joan, 118
Bobby Deerfield, 116
Boyd, Stephen, 63-4
Boyd William, 51, 53, 61
Brando, Marlon, 65
Brodie, Steve, 28
Broncho Billy, 46-8
"Broncho Billy," 30
Brooklyn Bridge Brodies, 28
Bullitt, 100, 109-13
Burgess, Earl, 68

Caan, James, 162
Cactus Cure, The, 57
Caddo Field, 81
California Board of Education, 162
Cannonball Run, 155
Canutt, Enos Edward (Yakima), 51, 53-65
Channing, Stockard, 132

Chaplin, Charlie, 32, 67
Charlie Varrick, 92
Chesty Anderson, U.S. Navy, 166
City on Fire, 151
"Cliff-hangers," 34
Code Red, 156
Comes a Horseman, 155
Conan, the Barbarian, 148
Cooper, Ken, 61-2
Cowboys, The, 15
"Cowgirls," 121
Crouper mount, 165

Dakota, 61
Danko, Betty, 118-21
Dawn Patrol, The, 83
Death Race 2000, 115-16
De Mille, Cecil B., 72
Dodge car stunts, 109, 117
Dressler, Marie, 41
Duncan, William, 102
Dunn, Bobby, 26

Earhart, Amelia, 86
Earthquake, 132, 166
Eastwood, Clint, 162
Edendale, L.A., 19-20, 22
Epper, Jeannie, 128, 132
Eyes of the Forest, 75

Fairbanks, Douglas, 31-2
Fields, W.C., 32, 106-07
Finn, Lila, 128, 132, 135
Five of Me, The, 157
Flight of the Phoenix, The, 89-90
Flowing Gold, 123
"Flying Fortress, The," 87
Flying Magazine, 69
Flynn, Errol, 47, 61
Fokker bomber stunts, 79-81
Fonda, Henry, 61, 151
Ford, John, 60
"Four Million Deaths and Four Men's Lives," 82
Friedkin, William, 26, 113-15
French Connection, The, 26, 100, 113-15

174

Index

Galloping Ghost, The, 84, 91
Garner, James, 162
Geary, Dick, 170
Gibson, Hoot, 40-1, 51
Gibson, Rose, 40-1
Girl at the Throttle, The, 40
Girl Telegrapher's Peril, The, 40
Gloria, 100
Goebel, Art, 76
Gone With The Wind, 61, 116
Gotha bombers, 81
Grace, Dick, 27, 73, 79-83
Great Gamble, The, 42
Great Stone Face, The, 28
Great Train Robbery, The, 66
Great Waldo Pepper, The, 92-9
Griffith, D.W., 19, 24, 67
Guinness Book of World Records, 11

Hagen, 115
Hal Roach Studios, 120
Handbury, Jim, 139
Hart, William S., 47-8
Hawks, 169
Hazards of Helen, The, 40
Helen of Troy, 63
Helen's Sacrifice, 40
Hell's Angels, 80-3, 86
Heston, Charlton, 63-5
Hickman, Bill, 110-15
High Point, 115, 137
Hindenberg, 149-50
Hollywood Stuntman, 16
Holmes, Helen, 40-1
"Honeymoon Express," 86
Hooper, 16
Hopalong Cassidy, 51, 61
Hughes, Howard, 80
"Human Rubber Ball, The," 29
Hurricane Hutch, 41
Hutchison, Charles, 41-4

Immelmann turn, 68
Intolerance, 24
It's a Mad Mad Mad Mad Mad World, 90
Ivanhoe, 63

Jennie Airplane stunts, 68, 75, 83, 92
Jesse James, 61
Johnson, Al, 81
Johnson, Julie, 128, 135-6
Jones, Buck, 51, 61
Joy of Living, 118

Kahana, Debbie, 166
Kahana, Kim, 161-68
Keaton, Buster, 28-9, 31-2, 67
Kelly, Patsy, 120
Keystone Company, 19-20
Keystone Kops, 20-1, 25, 101, 117, 152

"Kids Are People, Too," 166
King of Comedy, 19
"King of the Stunters," 73
King Richard and the Crusaders, 63
Knievel, Evel, 141
Knight, Arthur, 67
Knights of the Round Table, 63

Lafayette Escadrille, 90
Lawrence, Florence, 30
"Last Auto Race in the World, The," 107
Le Mans, 115-16
Lightning Hutch, 44
Lincoln car stunts, 94
Lindbergh, Charles, 84
"Little House on the Prairie," 166
Liveliest Art, The, 67
Lloyd, Harold, 29, 31-2
Locklear, Omar, 72-5
Loftin, Carey, 104-15, 139
Lord, Del, 25, 101, 117
Lost in the Jungle, 49
Lyons, Cliff, 61-2

Madison, Guy, 51, 61
Madison, Harry, 14, 159
Madsen, Harry, 159
Mann, Hank, 22, 32
Man of Conquest, 61
Mantz, Paul, 84-91, 93, 99
Matthau, Walter, 92
Maynard, Ken, 51, 61
McLaughlin, Ted, 73
Men With Wings, 86
Miller Brothers 1010 Ranch Show, 48
Mister Gunfighter, 15
Mix, Tom, 40, 48-51, 57, 75
Monroe, Marilyn, 128
Mother, Jugs and Speed, 135
Movieland of the Air Museum, 91
Ms. Magazine, 135
Murder, He Says, 120

Needham, Hal, 12, 153-54, 159, 171-72
New York Times, The, 99, 148, 155
Nieuport 28 plane stunts, 96
Nilsson, Anna Q., 123
Normand, Mabel, 27, 32

"108" Comic Fall, 28
Old Oklahoma, 61
O'Neil, Kitty, 9-12, 17, 128-32
On the Beach, 107-09, 112

Page, Grant, 149-52, 159
Paramount Pictures, 60, 78, 106, 120
Pearl White stunts, 36
Perfect Specimen, The, 118
Perkins, Gil, 53, 61

175

Index

Perils of Nyoka, The, 61
Perils of Pauline, The, 34-5, 44
Philadelphia balloon landing, 37
Photoplay Magazine, 82
Piper Aztec stunt, 99
Plunder, 37
Pontiac stunts, 113-14, 116-17
Professional Stuntmen's Federation, 173
"Process shots," 110
Pursued, 118

Raiders of the Lost Ark, 44-5
Ranch Life in the Great Southwest, 48
Redford, Robert, 92-9
Republic Pictures, 61
Reynolds, Burt, 17, 65, 116-17
Riders of the Dawn, 60
Ringel, "Jersey," 67
Robinson, Dar, 29, 138-43, 157, 159-60
Rocky, 116
Rocky Mountain, 47
Rogers, Buddy, 78
Rogers, Roy, 51, 60-1
Rogers, Will, 40
Roland, Ruth, 27, 39
Rollerball, 15
Romance and Rustlers, 57
Rose, Bob, 27, 39, 84, 90
"Running W," 55, 144-45
Rush, Loretta, 118, 123-24

San Francisco, 61
Saturday Evening Post, 131
Scott, Audry, 118-20, 125-28
Screen Actors Guild (SAG), 12, 156, 169, 170-71
Screen Extras Guild, 156
Secret of the Submarine, 101
Selig, William, 48-9
Sennett, Mack, 18-32
"Shock cord cable," 152
Sickle, Dale Van, 108-09
Sikorsky plane, 81
"Silent Victory: The Kitty O'Neil Story," 17
Skywayman, The, 69-73
Smokey and the Bandit, 116
Smokey and the Bandit II, 116-17
Society of Professional Stuntwomen, 172
Sopwith Camel plane stunts, 92
Spad airplane stunts, 79-81
Spy Smasher, 104
Stagecoach, 60
Stallone, Sylvester, 169
Standard plane stunts, 68, 92, 99
Steel, 155
Steerman biplane stunt, 84-5, 92
Sterling, Ford, 21-2

Stevens, Alex, 158, 160-61
Stevenson, John, 37-8
Sting, The, 116
Stolen Engine, The, 40
Stuntmen's Association of Motion Pictures, 170-71
Stunts Unlimited, 131, 171-72
Stuntwomen of America Organization, 132-35, 172
Such Men Are Dangerous, 83
Suicide Club, 77
"Suicide" initiation leap, 165
Summer Place, A, 128
Summerville, Slim, 27, 32
Sunset in El Dorado, 60
Sword and the Sorcerer, The, 156

Tallman, Frank, 90-9
Tanberg, Jack, 156
They Died With Their Boots On, 61
"They Kill Animals and They Call It Art," 148
Thirteen Flying Black Cats, 77
"Thrill-A-Minute Stunt King, The," 41-2
Tomick, Frank, 76-7
Towering Inferno, The, 149
Trail of the Lonesome Pine, 61
Trojan War film stunts, 63
True Confessions, 118
Turpin, Ben, 28, 32
Turner, Roscoe, 81, 83
Twelve Crowded Hours, 103-04
Twelve O'Clock High, 87
Twilight Zone, 90, 156
Two Minute Warning, 166

University of Texas Instruction for the Deaf, 128
Universal Studios, 125

Wake Me When It's Over, 90
Wayne, John, 51, 60-2
Welsh, Raquel, 135
Whirlwind, The, 42
White, Pearl, 34-5, 39
"Whoa!" stunt, 55
Wide Open, 76
Wiggins, Mary, 118, 121-23
Wild Bill Hickok westerns, 61
"Wildcats," 102
Wild Horse Canyon, 57
Wild Ones, The, 161
Williams, Esther, 128
Williams, Kathryn, 33, 49
Wilson, Al, 81-2
Wings, 78-82, 100
"Wonder Woman," 11, 129
World Wide Enterprises, 131

STUNT PEOPLE

George Sullivan & Tim Sullivan

It's easy to fall out of an airplane; it's hard to walk away unharmed. Stunt people are trained, professional actors who know how to perform impossible feats, and then, when their work is done, walk off the movie set in one piece.

From the Keystone Kops to *Raiders of the Lost Ark*, stunt people have made movie watchers forget their popcorn and chew their fingernails, sighing in relief or disbelief, as men and women fall down elevator shafts, roll cars over cliffs, and parachute into burning buildings so the movie stars remain unscarred.

In the days of silent movies there was very little technical know-how, no special training; only courage and agility helped stunt people perform their death-defying feats. Sometimes it wasn't enough. If D. W. Griffith, famous early filmmaker, needed someone to drive off a cliff, he found a race car driver who had enough confidence to do it. Today stunt people study science, physics, and mechanics. Technological advancements allow moviemakers to change the speed of the film, to drive cars with remote control, to make the stunt situation as safe as it can humanly be.

As Hal Needham, famous stand-in for